How to Be The One

by
Roy Sheppard

Centre Publishing,
Croft House, Clapton, Radstock, Bath
Somerset, BA3 4EB England.
Tel: 00 +44 (0) 1761 414541
Fax: 00 +44 (0) 1761 412615
Email: info@BeTheOneBook.com
Web: www.BeTheOneBook.com

First published in the United States in 2010

Library of Congress Cataloging-in-Publication Data
Sheppard, Roy
How to Be The One/Roy Sheppard. – 1st ed.

ISBN: 978-1901-534-139

Cover photograph © iStockPhotos.com/Irochka_T
Book design by Antony Parselle

Printed and bound in the USA

Thank you department

Single and married men and women from all over the world have helped me to develop many of the ideas I put forward in this book. Their invaluable insights, suggestions and a huge amount of encouragement are greatly appreciated.

This virtual team has been dotted around the UK, France, Germany, Russia, Hong Kong, the United States and Canada. What has struck me time and again is how everybody regardless of age, background, education or culture seems to share the same relationship issues and challenges. We all do the best we can. All relationships are hard. The best ones are harder still.

The following people have helped make this a better book. Thank you.

Toni Bailey, Martin Baldwin, Mark Bendle, Stephanie Bennett, Claire Cheung, Fiona David, Nicky Fussell, Emma Gordon-Stables, Kerry Hale, Henry Harington, Sally Helvey, Evgeny Lebedev, Rezwan Malik, Melissa Wadams & Vivienne Man at MoneyMadeClear.org.uk, Alexandra Massey, Shay and Margaret McConnon, Paul McGee, Anna Milone, Chris Moon MBE, Rebecca Murch, Antony Parselle, Allan and Barbara Pease, Deb Robertson, Bryan Sergeant, Glyn, Jill, Mike and Julie Sheppard, Pam and John Simonett, Paul Slater, Hilary Strickland, Caroline Talbott and Sarala Wadhwani.

Particular thanks to Nita Saini who has been such a star. Her contribution and insights have been incredibly valuable. And my dear friend Trish Bertram for our very long conversations about everything in this book and so much more. As ever, a massive thank you to Joe Robertson for his skills as an editor, his contributions, corrections and for his friendship.

John Gommes for his immense wisdom, stimulating conversation and support over the years. When it comes to being an outstanding mentor - he's 'The One'.

Finally, Richard Carlson PhD, for his outstanding and inspirational work. Following his untimely death in 2006, he has been sorely missed.

Contents

Preface

Bookshelves groan under the weight of books that explain how to get more dates or offer underhanded, dirty tricks and manipulative techniques readers can use to get their 'prey' to want them more, whether for casual sex or for marriage.

Some of these books boast sales in the millions and countless marriages as a result of their rules and deceitful techniques. The authors are less forthcoming about how many of those marriages actually ended in painful divorces for everyone, including countless innocent children.

Techniques to manipulate another individual may indeed work in the short term – but any relationship based on this type of behaviour cannot and will not last.

How to Be The One is **not** like those books. In these pages you will find hundreds of ways to become, without **any** manipulation or trickery, the sort of person another genuine man or woman would choose, and want to *keep* as a lifelong partner.

The key message throughout this book is a simple one. Although, it's easier to say than do. If you really want a long-term, meaningful relationship WITH the best, you have to be prepared to put some effort into BEING the best for them, too.

If you have already found 'The One', this book will also show you many ways to help you connect at a deeper level with your partner, especially if you read it together. It may also help rekindle the original love, respect and appreciation your relationship enjoyed in the past.

How to Be The One is also for the single men and women who are serious about wanting a long-term partner to share their lives with, in a special relationship based on honesty, kindness, mutual respect, deep intimacy and love, and are prepared to actually do something about it.

In fact, it's for anyone who wants to be that one person who brings out the best in a partner, who is in turn, as equally devoted to you.

All too often, when there's any discussion about relationships the focus is on the differences between the sexes. There are so many books, magazine articles, and radio and TV programmes on the subject. Some are divisive, driving a wedge between the sexes, while others such as those by Allan and Barbara Pease, offer valuable information communicated in an entertaining, engaging way.

This book sets out, in a gender-neutral way, to concentrate on the *similarities* and shared relationship aspirations of men and women of all ages and backgrounds. It has therefore been created following extensive collaboration with a team of men and women, both single and married. Rather than taking a group of women or men into a room and talking to them about what the other sex doesn't understand or consistently fails to get right, please think of this book as the equivalent of bringing men and women together into the same room, and discussing together how each gender can better understand the needs, fears and dreams of the other. Doing this, it is hoped that everyone can gain more clarity about what men and women look for in a long-term partner, and what YOU can do to become that person, whether for your existing partner, or for that special someone you have yet to meet. You may also become a far more appealing person to yourself.

How to Be The One is therefore very definitely for men and women.

Please make this book your own. Write in it. Answer the questions. Do the exercises. Jot down notes. Do whatever it takes to absorb the most relevant ideas. A tiny improvement today can have massive and positive effects in the longer term. And when you add together a lot of small improvements the benefits are even greater. A ship that alters its course by only one degree will, over time, end up in a totally different place. So can you. And it will be a better place.

Isn't it odd that we all seem to know what we need to do, but we don't do even the basics? In many cases the reason is simple – we forget. At the end of each Emotional Core section, you will find a series of daily Stop and Start Reminders to help you integrate new thoughts and behaviours into your life. You don't have to do **any** of them. Really. Because if you agree with any of what you read, and then think and feel it's a chore to make adjustments in your behaviour and attitude, you won't do it. You might start with good intentions but it probably won't last.

However, if you choose to make the Reminders a part of your future life, you will benefit more from the rest of what's in this book. Many of the ideas are so simple. When taken on their own, they may appear fairly small and insignificant. But add them all together, and apply them over time and they become a powerful and potent way to be far more appealing to others. There is space at the end of each section for you to add any new reminders you can think of.

You might choose to mark those reminders most relevant to you in the boxes alongside them. The more you remind yourself to make even small improvements on a daily basis, the more likely it will be that these actions will become new and beneficial habits. Repeated often enough, in time your brain learns to do them unconsciously. They become permanent improvements.

So when you read this book just **play** with any of the ideas it triggers. Play around with what you learn and what you **choose** to do. Carry the book with you. Dip into it on a regular basis. Then once you've read it, perhaps using a text highlighter pen too, you might want to make appointments in your diary to skim-read the book again weekly, or in a month's time, then a month or two after that.

One more thing - please don't **ever** beat yourself up about anything you read in this book. On that basis, you are invited to be The One for that special person you have either yet to meet, or perhaps you've already met – and you'd like them to choose to stay in your life forever.

If you find this book particularly thought-provoking and helpful, please discuss it with family, friends and partners. Be free to disagree. Use it as a springboard towards a better future for you. And for them.

I believe that everyone has all the answers. Seriously. But in many cases they aren't asking the most helpful questions. Most people get 'stuck' sometimes. Often this is because they keep asking themselves the same unhelpful questions. An unhelpful relationship question could be *"Will I EVER find 'The One'?"* A more helpful alternative could be *"I wonder what I could do right now, to increase the chances that I do meet 'The One' – and they feel the same way about me?"* That's what you'll find in this book – lots of new, empowering questions to trigger new thoughts and better options. Sometimes it can take just one breakthrough question that really hits home to have a miraculous and magical impact. Imagine how valuable it would be to you if you found a lot of really great questions here. With an open mind, you just might. And you might even find yourself being able to answer them.

You might be asking *"Who are you to be writing this book?"* Well, for the past 30 years I have earned a living 'on-stage', on TV or on the radio asking questions. I trained as a hypnotherapist. I have facilitated and moderated countless in-depth, highly-charged and sometimes highly-sensitive discussions. My role is to be an independent 'conscience of the audience' to bring together participants and audience members in order to gain greater clarity of thinking, a better understanding of the issues discussed and a shared desire to move forward in a constructive way. In many cases my questions can be pretty unpalatable, and often very challenging.

A UK journalist once described me as a 'business Oprah Winfrey', which I still think is a pretty cool compliment.

I've lectured and written extensively on creating and maintaining business as well as personal relationships at leading business schools, conferences and seminars. I've been interviewed on radio and TV about all facets of relationships more times than I can remember. And personally, I have been married and divorced twice. Therefore I am also a participant, not just an observer.

A First-Class You

When I was 24, I worked for the BBC. I was what is known as a 'Continuity Announcer'. Not only was I a 'voice of the BBC', with my role came a great deal of responsibility. I was personally responsible for putting television programmes on the air. More importantly, when things went wrong, as they often did in those days, I had the authority to make some fairly important decisions that affected the BBC. For a 24 year old, it was quite stressful. Because of this responsibility, and how the BBC was organised, I had a fairly senior management grade. And with that came a number of perks, one of which was being allowed to travel first class on the train, if I was travelling on BBC business. If you're a British reader you'll be pleased to know that I never wasted your TV licence fee* by doing so. I thought it was wrong.

Anyway, many years later I went through a personal crisis. The word 'divorce' was part of it (I told you I was a participant.) When you go through particularly bad times in your life, you tend to reflect on all sorts of things. What you've learned. What you'd do again. And what you wouldn't.

I found myself thinking about the real reason I never travelled first class when I worked at the BBC. In truth, I didn't feel I deserved to travel first class. You see, at that point, everything about my life was 'in economy'. I didn't feel I ever deserved anything better than 'cheap'. Certainly nothing first class. This hit me hard. For the next week or so, I found myself feeling very upset about this realisation.

Then one day, it dawned on me that 'first class' isn't a seat, it's an attitude. It's an attitude to life. Therefore, it's also a choice. I decided from that moment on to live a first-class life. There have certainly been times since then when I've forgotten to do so. But it's not long before I remember again and carry on with life.

I sincerely believe that you can also make the same choice. You can be first class. Simply by deciding to be first class. Not in a narcissistic, arrogant way, or insisting that you, or someone else, pay more than you need to for 'toys' that make you feel important – short term. But first class at a much deeper level. Being a first-class person for The One can only happen if you have made an investment in being a first-class person for yourself.

Every first-class athlete is aware of their 'Core'. 'Core' muscles reside deep inside the pelvis, lower back and abdomen. Athletes know how critically important these muscles are to their physical stability, flexibility and strength. All top-level training programmes include a regime to develop an athlete's 'Core'.

For the first time, this book introduces the concept of your Emotional Core. This consists of four core emotional qualities that help with your stability, depth, flexibility and inner-strength. A strong and robust Emotional Core effectively protects your heart, and even your soul.

The best relationships can be truly transformational, but we all know that a bad one can also be so devastating. For many, the pain of previous relationships exacts a high price. They feel unable or unwilling to surrender to the sheer joy of a relationship – just in case it doesn't work out and they end up 'falling apart'. So they enter all relationships (especially those they think could be significant ones) in a highly defensive manner.

However, a strong Emotional Core that has been developed over time, gives you the inner strength to know that even if you get injured emotionally, you are more likely to be able to cope effectively and also recover far more quickly. (This is precisely how athletes benefit following injury when they have a strong physical core.)

This isn't to suggest that you throw caution to the wind with everyone you meet. But knowing you have a strong Emotional Core allows you the opportunity to be emotionally available to your partner. Do that, and you become as irresistible to The One, as they are to you. And without any tricks, manipulation or deception. You just can't have a successful long-term relationship if it's based on 'faking it'.

How to Be The One is about how you can become a first class version of **you**. It doesn't mean 'perfect' because no one is – and those who insist on perfection for themselves invariably make life fairly miserable for everybody else around them.

I hope this book proves to be a first-class ticket for your future journey.

Roy Sheppard. Bath, England. July 2010.

*For non-UK readers, in Britain you have to pay an annual licence fee to own or rent a TV set. Revenue from this licence fee is currently used to fund production of all BBC radio and television programmes.

Chapter 1

First-Class Choice

1989. *When Harry Met Sally* was a sensationally successful movie. Starring Meg Ryan as Sally and Billy Crystal as Harry, it told the story of how two people meet, **don't** fall in love, yet eventually come to realise that they are 'The One' for each other. It's most memorable and hilarious scene was probably Sally faking an orgasm, sitting at a table in a diner. And even now, after all these years, I still crack up at that comment from the older woman sitting nearby: *"I'll take what she's having."*

I also remember the film for a very short scene where their mutual friend Marie (played by Carrie Fisher) is sitting up in bed with her husband, Jess, talking about 'being single'. She says: *"Tell me I'll never have to be out there again."* Jess looks into her eyes and says: *"You'll never have to be out there again."* Just about everyone in a really happy and successful relationship 'gets' what they are saying.

Being single can be fantastic. For some, but not everyone. It can be fun and exciting. There's the independence and the choices: bars, parties, clubs, drink, drugs, hot dates and even hotter, steamy sex. You're free to do what, and who, you please. Getting drunk. Getting laid. Maybe wishing you hadn't. And promising yourself that it won't happen so easily the next time. And all those other things you don't tell your parents. Whatever you want is certainly out there somewhere. And there are a helluva lot of people you can do it with.

'The Moment'

Then one day, most normal men and women, wake up feeling as if they're 'velcroed to the mattress', utterly exhausted from whatever they got up to the previous night. They experience 'The Moment'. It's that glimmer of a realisation that the constant partying isn't *quite* as much fun as it used to be. And that, perhaps – just perhaps, it might be time to find someone special to be with, long term. If you've had 'The Moment', you'll know exactly what I mean.

As we saw in the movie, Sally was brilliant at 'faking it'. This book isn't about faking anything. It's about being honest with yourself and respectful of others. It's about being The One, being special and **ready** for the time when you meet that person (if you haven't done so already). Or perhaps, like Harry and Sally you have, but don't realise it yet.

How to Be The One is about what you can do - ethically - to increase the chances that The One you choose is The One who also chooses you, for the long term, and all in an honest, kind and loving way.

The rest of this chapter is specifically written for single people, but if you're already in a relationship, go ahead and read it to learn what it's **really** like 'out there'. And how the world has changed so massively even since 1989 *When Harry Met Sally.*

Supply and Demand

In the business world, there's a law of 'supply and demand'. Basically, whenever there's a shortage of any resource (in this case, available single people), its value (or perceived value) goes up. For example, if there are only three people to choose from in your village, your choices of a mate are fairly limited – and so are theirs. You might hold out for someone better, but there could come a time when you are forced to face reality and lower your standards, rather than be alone. It's harsh, but that's what happened in previous centuries. And it still happens in many less-developed countries today.

It's one of the arguments in favour of arranged marriages. Families know each other, make a match (without using a dating website!), the couples get to know each other as friends, get married and live happily ever after. OK, that's just the theory – but there's quite a bit of research to suggest that a significant proportion of arranged marriages do actually work – for the men and the women.

Of course, there are also deeply unhappy men and women, trapped in loveless marriages, based on convenience rather than choice. But in many other cases, millions choose to work at it together to create really happy lives together. And for the sake of balance - if you want a comparison, talk to the 2 million or so Americans who end up in the divorce courts – *every year*!

The West ain't necessarily best!

In the past, you took what was on offer, made the most of it, or you went without.

But the flip side of the economic theory is also true, and much more relevant to any readers of this book who are currently single: a glut of any resource (such as available singles) makes the perceived value of each individual go down. When you're one of just a few choices, you don't have to bother that much. But when you're competing with so many really hot, active, enthusiastic and 'beautiful' people, the stakes are a lot higher. You need to put in at least some effort to improve your perceived value.

You can't expect to 'get' the best without working at 'being the best'. This book shows you how to stack the odds in your favour – without resorting to any dirty tricks.

The world has changed. Expect it to change even further. The 'Supply and Demand' equation is completely different, too. Populations have exploded everywhere. There are now more young single people on this planet than **ever** before. So the chances of getting a date have never been better. That's the plus side. But the downside is worth thinking about as well: the chances of not being asked out on a second date have never been higher, either. This isn't being negative, it's facing the hard facts.

The number of single people is predicted to rise even further in the next couple of decades. Add to that a large global population 'bulge' of people in their 40s-60s. These are the baby boomers. Many are re-entering the singles world in their middle age following a divorce. This means there's now a massive oversupply of single, available men and women of all ages.

With so many available people, competition for the best people has never been so high. And it will almost certainly intensify. Making sure you have the qualities you seek in others will therefore become more and more important. And that's not the same as making it just 'look' as if you have those qualities.

How Do Others Judge YOU?

The biggest potential problem going into a relationship is that the person you fall for doesn't feel the same way about you. And in today's world of unlimited choice, this is becoming more and more commonplace. With so many millions of single people out there, it has never been so easy to move on to the next person, just in case there's someone 'better'.

American comedian Chris Rock gets a huge laugh when he tells his audiences: *"Guys, no matter who you are, you are* ***NEVER*** *her first choice!"* Maybe that's a bit too true for comfort! And with so much choice, men can now afford to be more choosy too.

This book is designed to help you look at your own situation and behaviour in a different way. Not necessarily a 'better' way – just different. By thinking differently, you may choose to make different decisions about what you do, which in turn will affect how others respond to you. We all possess a collection of beliefs, attitudes, habits and other behaviours. Individually, they might not make much difference to who you are. However, the people we meet and become close to often notice (consciously or unconsciously) 'clusters' of these traits. It's the combination of these 'clusters' that lead to someone deciding, whether you are wildly or mildly appealing, or mildly or wildly unappealing. Helping you to think more constructively about who you are today, and who you can become tomorrow, can and will make a massive difference to your life. From the inside out.

It's the stuff you cannot see. It's what makes you irresistible – in a genuine way.

You probably have your own requirements in a partner. It might even be a long list. How many times have you pulled the plug on a relationship with someone who was really into you, but there was something 'not quite right' about them? Best keep looking, just in case!

Maybe as you read this, you're not quite ready to settle down with The One. Although when they appear, you might change your mind very quickly! Wouldn't it be a tragedy if that person continued their search, because you weren't providing the very qualities you valued so highly in others?

Everybody seems to want more from the people they meet and date. And yet most of us are only prepared to give more emotionally after getting what we want! We've all been hurt, so holding back is probably 'safer', isn't it? Unfortunately it doesn't quite work like that.

As you read the following chapters ask yourself this question: *"If I was in court accused of failing to provide each quality I require in others, would there be enough evidence for me to be convicted?"*

The 'Next' Generation

Thanks to the internet, being single has opened up mind-boggling opportunities to meet so many other single people. In one way, it is intoxicatingly exciting. It's just like being given the keys to the largest sweet shop in the world. But in another way, it can be utterly overwhelming – even frightening. Far too much choice leads to a level of disposability that is difficult to manage. Meet someone who isn't 'perfect'? A replacement is only a few clicks away.

The trouble with being part of the 'Next Generation' is how many times you say, or hear, the word 'Next'!

So if you're thinking: *"Surely, The One will take me just as they find me, warts and all"*... maybe. But what if the situation were reversed? Would you be that interested in someone who made no effort to meet your standards? And if you did, wouldn't you be likely to take a little peek around to see if someone 'better' was available? Why do you think they wouldn't do the same?

It's human nature.

I interviewed one particular young woman for this book. She said: *"But why should I be the one to change? If he loved me, he'd take me as I am."* In reality, when there are this many available people to choose from, the highest calibre people can afford to be extremely selective. They can 'try before they buy' as often as they like. And anyone who fails to meet those standards in any way, is gone. It's as simple as that. My answer to that young woman was: *"You don't **have** to change at all. Although if you want to attract (and keep) the best, you might decide that 'becoming the best you can be' is at least worth considering."*

Doesn't it therefore make sense to think about what you most want in a long-term partner and make damn sure you have the same qualities you regard as so essential in others? You can be pretty sure they will keep searching until they find someone with the qualities they regard as essential. When it really comes down to it, it's not just about the clothes they wear, how well they keep in shape or the car they drive. It's about the person they are inside. And it is what is inside of you that they will be looking for... and assessing and, yes, even judging. And they may not judge it very favourably if you expect them to love you unconditionally, without making any effort to appeal to them.

You want someone kind, perhaps. How prepared are you to be at least as kind? It's the same with every other quality you would want in a future partner or spouse. Those in good relationships devote themselves to bringing out the best in each other, in equal measure. This is fundamental to the success of any long-term relationship. If one person does all the giving, while the other does the 'taking', it's only a matter of time before that relationship will become strained or broken.

Someone will become the 'ex' in 'n-ex-t'.

Internet Dating

The average length of a relationship started via a UK dating website is about seven months according to research by Bath Spa University in the UK. Not exactly permanent is it? There are just too many 'hot' people to date. Is this heaven? Or is it dating hell? That depends a lot on your mindset.

These issues don't only affect young singles either. Louise is in her early forties. She finally plucked up courage to join a dating site after a painful and protracted divorce. She's a genuinely attractive woman. Her online profile photo was just a quick snapshot: no special lighting, no professional make-up or hairstylist. Within just 48 hours of uploading her profile, she received 183 emails from men (and a few women!). She was totally overwhelmed. Too overwhelmed in fact. She nailed it when she told me: *"I was 'new meat'."*

She didn't want to be 'new meat'. She wanted a 'new meet', a genuine guy to get to know and to love – and be loved. She didn't want to be part of what she described as 'this feeding frenzy'. How many of those 183 men could have been The One? Who will ever know? In truth probably, not that many.

As Louise found, the choice 'out there' can be SO huge, it is becoming very difficult to sift the good from the bad. Who hasn't scanned endless profile pages, instantly dismissing people based on a tiny photo and a few sentences they've written about themselves or had written by a friend? And they are making split-second decisions in exactly the same way about you. Except the 'creepy' ones of course: they *always* seem to want to get in touch with you. In much the same way as the comedian Jasper Carrott observed that the 'nutter' on the bus *always* wants to talk to you - not anybody else!

Does that mean dating sites are a waste of time for anyone who is serious about meeting someone special? Absolutely not.

Dating sites are without doubt the most fantastic and effective way that has ever been invented to connect with a lot of single people who have all decided to tell the world that they are 'available'. Although don't forget that there are still so many other effective ways to meet available single people offline, too. But to give you a sense of how many websites there are, for a fairly comprehensive listing visit www.BeTheOneBook.com

Let's look at this phenomenon a bit closer and look at the numbers, to understand the sheer scale of internet dating today.

Match.com has more than 16 million American members (15% of the 95.9 million unmarried adults in the US). In the UK there are an estimated 15 million single people, a third of whom are registered with at least one UK dating website. Study the business predictions for companies like Meetic, which owns DatingDirect.com, the UK's largest dating website (5 million members), and Match.com in Europe, and you'll see growth. Business is excellent in the online dating world because demand is so huge. And it's set to rise even further. Which is precisely why new dating websites keep popping up everywhere, aimed specifically at satisfying the needs of just about every definable group of single people; based on locality, race, age, colour, religious beliefs, hobbies, income and sexual preferences.

But it's in China where the singles market is really exploding. Chinese website Zhenai.com is the largest dating site in the world with over 22 million members, followed closely by Jiayuan.com. It's estimated that there will be 140 million singles in China sometime soon. Adding any more numbers here is pointless since, by the time you read this, they'll have changed. But one thing is for sure, the numbers will have gone up.

And it's a similar story in just about every developed country in the world: more single people than ever before. Quite simply, there have never been so many opportunities to meet anyone, for anything. And that includes The One.

Searching profiles online can be strangely addictive. Receiving a constant stream of emails from seemingly attractive men and women is also exciting and great for the self-esteem. Whether it helps you find The One is a different matter though.

Being less than honest about yourself in your profile has even become an expected part of the internet dating experience. But it's hardly the basis for a solid long-term relationship.

All too often, the online promise is far more appealing than the reality, as anyone who has dated someone 20 years older or 40 pounds heavier than their picture, will tell you.

Stories abound too of male and female 'serial internet daters', constantly searching for the next date, and the next and the next. And as you may have already discovered if you use online dating sites, there are also a significant number of people who don't ever get around to actually meeting anyone face-to-face. With so many to choose from online, it's good enough for them just to feel wanted. Who knows how many of these men and women aren't even single, feeling trapped in a mundane marriage? You can lead a double life having a string of non-affairs. Online cheating in their minds is perhaps better than real cheating. And there are the ex-girlfriends and ex-boyfriends who take on the persona of a fictitious person in order to make contact with their former partners and keep up with what they are doing, so they can hate them from afar. There are some very strange people in cyberspace.

But what else can you do, when you are always only a click away from being rejected?

With so many available people to choose from, how do you manage the scale of the opportunity? Why not pack in as many dates as you can? The 'Speed dating' concept was born. It makes so much sense, too. But only if you're into quantity not quality. According to conventional wisdom, humans make up their minds about someone within three minutes. So, on that basis, it makes perfectly good sense to have as many three minute dates as possible. It's an excellent business model for speed dating companies, too. Even when you don't find anyone, you keep coming back 'just in case'.

On the one hand, there are huge opportunities to meet available men and women. Whilst on the other, it's become so easy (in many ways, far too easy) to give up on someone, or for that someone else to give up on you. As the aptly named website states, there are 'PlentyofFish' out there.

Throwing a tasty fish back, just in case there's a better one swimming nearby, is too tempting for so many. (Now you know why there's a fish on this book cover.) The One that got away is always a great fishing story, but makes for a lousy dating story. How many 'Ones' have you already thrown back, perhaps for minor reasons?

Intimacy

Joining any dating website or speed dating group says: *"I am looking for intimacy."* Some want depth, while others choose to stay in the 'shallow' end of the intimacy pool. Everybody wants intimacy. It's a basic psychological need for all humans. Whether that need is for the short, medium or long term.

Sociologists predict that loneliness and isolation will become the most common psychological 'disease' of the 21st century. Which is really odd if you think about it because how can you be lonely when it has also been predicted that the global population could be eight billion in the next 20 years. And about a third of all adults will be single.

Definitions of intimacy vary widely of course; from the desire to mate for life with one partner and share the deepest forms of intimacy with that one person, to no-strings attached 'intimate' sex with as many strangers as possible. And it's not just the men. During research for this book, numerous women have admitted they use the web primarily to satisfy their sexual needs.

What is your personal definition of intimacy? How deep do you want it to be and, in an ideal world, how long would you like it to last? My guess is that the fact that you are reading this book means you want longer-term intimacy with one special person.

The key of course is being able to figure out from all of the individuals you meet or date, which ones share your precise definition of intimacy, are emotionally available to you and are actually telling you the truth.

Anyone who has been (or is still) in a 'one-night stand' phase of their life will often admit that casual sex gives them a form of short-lived intimacy. Men like the idea they have what it takes to 'pull' (to 'get the girl'), while women who have sex with these strangers, may not choose this option, but at least they feel 'wanted' – even if it's just for a few minutes. Dulling the 'pain' of the fake intimacy of a one-night stand often requires copious 'medication' in the form of recreational drugs or booze. And thick 'beer goggles' of course.

The fantastically talented singer Lily Allen summed this up so perfectly in the lyrics of her song *22*. She sings about a woman who just wants a boyfriend – but all she gets is one-night stands. She captures the quiet desperation of someone who appears to have everything on the surface but has nothing deep inside. The tragedy behind her lyrics is particularly poignant for a growing number of women. And men too.

There is a funny side as well. One woman in an interview for this book, claimed that she had never had a one-night stand. She added with a mischievous smile: *"The guy **always** calls!"* I nearly choked on my coffee as I realised she meant she was that good in bed!

Auditions for Intimacy

A date is nothing more than a formal 'Audition for Intimacy'.

Any actor will tell you that you don't get a role without attending auditions. And you don't succeed at auditions unless you've done your preparation. In my past, even though I was never an actor, I attended many auditions for roles in TV commercials and presenter jobs on TV. In one day, I was actually rejected for being the wrong sex, the wrong age, the wrong colour and the wrong height. Talk about not being Mr Right.

My agent once put me up for the role of a journalist in a real Hollywood blockbuster, *Patriot Games* starring Harrison Ford. They were looking for someone to play a BBC reporter, delivering a 'piece to camera' outside a hospital. The casting director was keen for me to meet the director, Phillip Noyce, because I was a genuine BBC news presenter at the time.

I was asked back three times to deliver my 20 seconds of dialogue, once on the movie set at Pinewood Studios. This alone was a childhood dream come true for me regardless of whether I got the role. How excited and petrified was I? A small speaking role in a major Hollywood blockbuster...and I was on a shortlist of two. Wow.

The excitement, expectation and attention of the movie business is quite intoxicating. A lot like dating in fact. And so is the rejection. Sadly, *Patriot Games* had to be 'carried' by Harrison Ford without my contribution. That role went to a woman playing the role of a CNN reporter.

In the media world, you learn to deal with rejection quite quickly, or you find another profession. Rejection isn't personal... it just feels that way. It can be soul-destroying, but it's the same with dating, isn't it?

I was right for that part. I wanted that part. But it didn't happen. Again, just like dating sometimes.

No matter how talented (or even how famous) you are, actors and other professional performers know that no one gets every job or part they 'go up for'. Countless talented people routinely hear those dreaded words 'Next!' Many actors keep going to auditions for years. For most, auditions are deeply unpleasant, angst-ridden affairs. Few professionals enjoy them. All the while, they prepare themselves for that brief moment when they might get their big break. Just like dating again?

The old Hollywood studio system identified raw talent and then taught these actors their craft: how to walk, talk, not bump into the furniture and look their best. If a future happy relationship is truly important to you, how much are you willing to prepare for what might become the most important 'Audition for Intimacy' you ever attend?

Recently I watched the entire *Godfather* movie trilogy. At the time these movies came out they were regarded as particularly violent. They don't seem to be any more, when you compare them with what is available now. Part of the box-set included a bonus DVD which included a lot of interview material with director Francis Ford Coppola and his team of actors. It was so fascinating watching the actual filmed auditions by young relatively unknown actors: Al Pacino, Robert De Niro, Diane Keaton, Robert Duvall and James Caan. Coppola spotted this raw talent and cast them in roles which ultimately catapulted them all to international fame and fortune. I was so struck at how important these short auditions turned out to be for the future careers of these actors. Their lives changed forever once they were awarded these roles.

Those actors (and every other performer who has ever attended an audition) prepared for those auditions by working at their craft so they were ready when opportunity came knocking on their door. As the saying goes: *"Sometimes it takes years to become an overnight sensation."*

Yet, who hasn't watched at least one of the many TV talent shows where tens of thousands of aspiring stars of all ages try their luck by attending open auditions. In many cases, queues stretch around the block as these wannabes wait in line for their 'big break'. This is 'Speed Dating On Stage On Steroids'. In less than three minutes you get the chance to impress those steely-eyed casting directors. Exactly like speed dating.

Those who just show up 'for a laugh' rarely, if ever, get far. And they **never** win. Winners are always incredibly focused, passionate, dedicated, committed, talented and they are always **ready**.

How Ready Do You Want to Be?

Wanting the best available partner is perfectly natural. This has been the case for centuries. There's nothing new about that. But what is new is how our expectations have changed and what we have come to believe a good relationship is based on.

This was very well illustrated in a *Daily Mail* article by romantic fiction author Josephine Cox. In *Read My Lips! Love Stories are Just a Con* (25 October 2007) she recounted a conversation she overheard between two women in their mid to late twenties. One was telling the other about a guy she'd been seeing, who was great fun to be with, who treated her particularly well and always ensured she got home safely. But then she added: *"I couldn't ever go out with a man who has crooked teeth. They aren't even that white."*

I wonder how long it will be before that woman realises that kindness and character are perhaps a tad more important than straight, whiter-than-white teeth. As her body clock starts to tick more loudly in the years to come, will she find herself 'settling' for a guy with a dazzling smile but who treats her poorly?

In that article, Cox, a multi-million selling romantic fiction writer, went on to reflect on how she and other writers like her could be to blame for creating and perpetuating wholly unrealistic expectations about romantic love, and those perfect, chivalrous, passionate, chisel-jawed, six-pack laden hunks. In all those passionate affairs, the relationships just happen. Happiness is always assured. Reality is never permitted to intrude. And Hollywood feeds the world with the same myths. Everyone is perfect, and everything always turns out well in the final five minutes. Happiness is guaranteed – without any effort or commitment. We'll explore these very issues in Chapter 11: TLC - Trust, Love and Commitment.

So how do you fit into this, whether you are married, living with a partner or as a single person, at whatever age you are, young or back out on the dating scene again following a break up or divorce? That is what the following chapters are about: helping you highlight what is most appealing about yourself, and working on reducing or even eliminating what's less appealing.

Chapter 2

Project You

A woman goes over to a guy in a pub. She says: *"I haven't seen you in here before. Are you local?"* In a slightly slurred voice he replies: *"No, actually I've just come out of prison. I served a 25 year sentence for chopping up my wife into tiny pieces."*

She says: *"So you're single then?"*

Hot and Spicy Food For Thought

In Britain, the national dish seems to have become Chicken Tikka Masala. We like our food hotter and spicier. And sometimes away from home. The same goes for many of our relationships. A curry may be exciting and more stimulating to the taste buds but remember this true fact: curries came about as a way of using hot spices to disguise poor quality, even rotting meat. A perfect relationship analogy don't you think? How often have you (or one of your friends) been in the early stages of a very spicy relationship only to discover after some steamy sex that the spice had cleverly obscured a really rotten person behind it?

Perhaps this is the real difference between 'fun dates' and building a lasting relationship with The One. Fun dates tend to start 'hot', progress to 'warm', and then on to 'cold'. Often within a few short, but spicy, hours, days, weeks or months.

By contrast, long-lasting relationships invariably start far slower, moving from cold, to warm, to slightly warmer still, to hot, and on to sizzling. The best relationships continue to 'simmer' for years and years. Could it be that all the effort to be 'hot', or 'have' hot at the outset might just be what's not working for you – and millions of others?

A happy, long-lasting relationship is more like a casserole than a spicy curry. Boring by comparison, casseroles are cooked at a lower heat over a longer time, when even the toughest ingredients will be made tender and succulent, nourishing the soul, and warming the heart. Especially on a cold winter's day. And, it has to be said, with a casserole, you never quite know what will next appear on your fork.

Our relationship with food can tell us so much about ourselves and what drives us. Fast, hot and spicy? Is quantity more important than quality? Healthy versus junk? Do you eat to nourish your body or are you a slave to your taste buds? Prepared from scratch or convenient from a packet? In times of stress and feeling upset, how often is food used to comfort you? Is food one of the forms of 'medication' you use to feel better about yourself? Is one of your closest friends called 'chocolate'? Do you stop eating when you're full, or do you keep going? And do you later get upset that you couldn't stop yourself? Or do you have a history of starving yourself of food for any number of other reasons?

How does your relationship with food provide possible insights about how you relate to people, especially those on an intimate basis?

We expect our food to be very tasty. Indeed bland is seen by many as bad, even boring. Interestingly, when you cook food grown yourself, as I do, you tend to add salt and pepper more sparingly. Homemade tomato soup, for example, has a far more subtle taste. You learn to savour that subtlety, yet when you share with friends, real home-grown, home-made food you often get a nervously asked: *"Do you have any salt?"*

It doesn't actually need salt, but we are now so conditioned to intensify the flavours of everything in our lives. Subtlety is lost. If it's subtle and slow – forget it. If food or life isn't packed with flavour, it will be 'improved' and speeded up in whatever ways possible. Again, a bit like some new relationships, don't you think?

In Europe, food is fuel for conversation. In America, food tends to be just fuel; the only country whose culinary contribution to global cuisine is serving food in a bucket! In Asia, food is revered. Rice is the 'soul' of every meal. All other ingredients accompany the rice. Westerners tend to view the meat and vegetables as the main dish, while the rice (the soul) is eaten as the accompaniment.

Asian food has become enormously popular around the world. Yet how many times does it get gulped down so quickly, amidst animated conversation with friends who are so distracted, they barely notice the food? At best, if someone asks what they think of it, the response may be limited to an enthusiastic: *"It's really nice. Very tasty."* They might even add: *"We should come here again."* Like some relationships.

Few westerners in particular, fully appreciate the sheer artistry and sophistication of a well-prepared Asian meal. Using only the best, freshest ingredients, a chef will combine, sometimes in the most sublime way, hot, sweet, sour, bitter and salty flavours. All the flavours are there in absolute harmony. The perfect relationship. No one flavour is allowed to overpower all the others. Simultaneously, the same ingredients are also chosen for their aromatic properties. On top of all that, ingredients are included to add visual stimulation: red, yellow, green and orange vegetables complete the sensory experience.

So the next time you have an Asian meal, especially Thai, Malaysian or Vietnamese cuisine – really slow down. Savour the moment and appreciate it fully. It's in moments like that, when you taste life itself.

For at least the next week, eat every meal sitting down (and not at your desk!) and eat it slowly. Notice how your appreciation for food goes up. You will find that you actually meet yourself. You may also find that you feel full before you've eaten everything on your plate. Then stop. (So you could even lose some excess weight, too.) And if you don't already do this, devote at least one evening per week (as a start) to making a healthy meal from scratch. No convenience packets. Buy fresh ingredients. After all, you've probably already accumulated enough celebrity cookbooks. This tip is particularly relevant to men. A man who can cook demonstrates depth of character and shows that he knows how to look after himself. A man who doesn't, is less appealing to a woman because if he can't look after himself, there's not much chance he'll bother to look after her either.

Let's Shop

"Be Proactive" and *"Begin with the end in mind"* are the first and second of Stephen Covey's *Seven Habits of Highly Effective People*. So, let's do that right now.

Just for fun, imagine you're going shopping for the perfect 'One'. This doesn't work in the real world, but it's a fantastic way to look at your own priorities, beliefs, values and what is really important to you in a partner, rather than what you might believe is important at the moment.

Think of this exercise as choosing the best quality, fresh ingredients you can find to make the most outstanding gourmet meal you've ever prepared – The One is on the menu. You are putting this together based on your own existing recipe. This might well change, but when you know your preferred ingredients, instant changes can be made which still produce a tasty, heart-warming and nourishing result. Can't cook (yet)? In such cases, we are often tempted to take the quickest, easiest options; invariably the brightly coloured, ready packed convenient alternatives. They're designed to get our attention. It works. But what's inside isn't always of the highest quality. Like potential partners.

When we go to a supermarket, we don't pick one of

everything that's on offer, we're selective. Although less selective than we might think. Purely from habit, lack of time or brand preference, we often choose the same or similar products most of the time. And, we do it in a mildly hypnotic state, not always consciously aware of what we're doing. We like to think our choices are based on logic – the retail experts know that just isn't so!

So, on your quest for the perfectly matched, most compatible man or woman, below you'll see a comprehensive list of everything on offer by the supermarket – a bit like what you're confronted with if you've ever done your shopping online. It's quite a long list. Don't be overwhelmed. Take your time. And try to avoid choosing items just because you've bought them in the past.

For your convenience and for added efficiency, the list has been arranged as aisles to emulate the layout of this make-believe supermarket.

To continue the shopping analogy. How many men and women wrongly think they've been left on the shelf? Or that they're past their sell-by date, condemned to the bargain-basement section?

One more thing: while you're walking the aisles during this shopping trip, picking and choosing the qualities you **most** want in a perfect partner, that actual person is also shopping for their perfect partner, too.

Step 1

Which of the qualities below would you most want in your partner? Be selective. At least for a moment, think about each one before you put a tick in the box alongside each quality. For the moment, ignore the numbers on the right. I'll explain what you do with those after your shopping trip.

You've got your shopping cart. And you've actually got one without a wonky wheel. It could be a 'sign' of good things to come. So let's shop.

Aisle 1 - Attitude Towards Life

Character Trait	✓	0 Not at all - 10 Top marks										
Passionate about life		0	1	2	3	4	5	6	7	8	9	10
Patient		0	1	2	3	4	5	6	7	8	9	10
Relaxed		0	1	2	3	4	5	6	7	8	9	10
Playful		0	1	2	3	4	5	6	7	8	9	10
Spontaneous		0	1	2	3	4	5	6	7	8	9	10
Fun-loving		0	1	2	3	4	5	6	7	8	9	10
Upbeat and Positive		0	1	2	3	4	5	6	7	8	9	10
Energetic		0	1	2	3	4	5	6	7	8	9	10
Easy-going		0	1	2	3	4	5	6	7	8	9	10

Aisle 2 - Attitude Towards Self

Character Trait	✓	0 Not at all - 10 Top marks										
Respect for self		0	1	2	3	4	5	6	7	8	9	10
Healthy self-esteem		0	1	2	3	4	5	6	7	8	9	10
Depth of character		0	1	2	3	4	5	6	7	8	9	10
Confident		0	1	2	3	4	5	6	7	8	9	10
Prepared to be wrong		0	1	2	3	4	5	6	7	8	9	10
Honest		0	1	2	3	4	5	6	7	8	9	10
Exercises regularly		0	1	2	3	4	5	6	7	8	9	10

Aisle 3 - Attitude Towards a Partner

Character Trait	✓	0 Not at all - 10 Top marks										
Romantic		0	1	2	3	4	5	6	7	8	9	10
Good companion		0	1	2	3	4	5	6	7	8	9	10
A calming influence		0	1	2	3	4	5	6	7	8	9	10
Supportive		0	1	2	3	4	5	6	7	8	9	10
Sexually passionate		0	1	2	3	4	5	6	7	8	9	10
Loyal		0	1	2	3	4	5	6	7	8	9	10
Understanding		0	1	2	3	4	5	6	7	8	9	10
Good listener		0	1	2	3	4	5	6	7	8	9	10

Aisle 4 - Mental Attitude

Character Trait	✓	0 Not at all - 10 Top marks										
Thoughtful		0	1	2	3	4	5	6	7	8	9	10
Wise		0	1	2	3	4	5	6	7	8	9	10
Humble		0	1	2	3	4	5	6	7	8	9	10
Committed		0	1	2	3	4	5	6	7	8	9	10
Pragmatic		0	1	2	3	4	5	6	7	8	9	10
Energetic		0	1	2	3	4	5	6	7	8	9	10
Spiritual		0	1	2	3	4	5	6	7	8	9	10

Aisle 5 - Emotional Attitude

Character Trait	✓	0 Not at all - 10 Top marks										
Loving		0	1	2	3	4	5	6	7	8	9	10
Compassionate		0	1	2	3	4	5	6	7	8	9	10
Happy		0	1	2	3	4	5	6	7	8	9	10
Generous		0	1	2	3	4	5	6	7	8	9	10
Appreciative		0	1	2	3	4	5	6	7	8	9	10
Emotionally Open		0	1	2	3	4	5	6	7	8	9	10

Aisle 6 - Attitude Towards Work

Character Trait	✓	0 Not at all - 10 Top marks										
Successful in Life		0	1	2	3	4	5	6	7	8	9	10
Hardworking		0	1	2	3	4	5	6	7	8	9	10
Well organised		0	1	2	3	4	5	6	7	8	9	10
Solution-focused		0	1	2	3	4	5	6	7	8	9	10
Creative		0	1	2	3	4	5	6	7	8	9	10
Savvy and smart		0	1	2	3	4	5	6	7	8	9	10
Forward thinking		0	1	2	3	4	5	6	7	8	9	10
Level of integrity		0	1	2	3	4	5	6	7	8	9	10
Trustworthy		0	1	2	3	4	5	6	7	8	9	10

Aisle 7 - Attitude Towards Others

Character Trait	✓	0 Not at all - 10 Top marks										
Helpful		0	1	2	3	4	5	6	7	8	9	10
Kind		0	1	2	3	4	5	6	7	8	9	10
Considerate		0	1	2	3	4	5	6	7	8	9	10
Friendly		0	1	2	3	4	5	6	7	8	9	10
Honourable		0	1	2	3	4	5	6	7	8	9	10

Aisle 8 - Attitude Towards Ideas

Character Trait	✓	0 Not at all - 10 Top marks										
Open- minded		0	1	2	3	4	5	6	7	8	9	10
Non-judgmental		0	1	2	3	4	5	6	7	8	9	10
Respect for others		0	1	2	3	4	5	6	7	8	9	10
Gracious		0	1	2	3	4	5	6	7	8	9	10
Fair-minded		0	1	2	3	4	5	6	7	8	9	10
Encouraging		0	1	2	3	4	5	6	7	8	9	10
Selfless		0	1	2	3	4	5	6	7	8	9	10

Step 2

OK, you've made your selection. Now it's time to study what you've chosen. Go back to the first item you selected and one-by-one, think carefully about each character trait you value so much in others. Then rate yourself for each of those qualities you've selected. For example, if you chose 'kindness' as a quality, how kind are you? If 'honesty' in others is really important to you, how honest are you? Be honest with yourself. No one else needs to see what you put.

After you've finished this part of your shopping, there's another very powerful stage. Although it's not for the faint-hearted. So don't read ahead yet. You'll spoil it.

You've now done your shopping for the perfect mate. Your trolley is full of all the qualities you most want and value in another person. And you've taken some time to rate yourself. You're feeling quite pleased with yourself, too. And you've rated yourself fairly highly on quite a few of the critical qualities you require in others.

You have now arrived at the supermarket checkout.

Standing at the next checkout is someone who has caught your eye. They're not your 'type' as such, but there is definitely something about them that you feel drawn to. Without knowing it, you are perfect for each other. Really. This match could only have been made in heaven. You have been brought together in this moment. You can't see what's in their trolley and they can't see what's in yours. The qualities most important to you are also incredibly important to them. What differences there are between you, make you ***perfectly*** compatible.

OK, so they aren't exactly like what you had on your list and they're not as tall as you're looking for. They don't look perfect. But they are perfect for you. You catch each other's eye. Both of you even give a watery half-smile. Unknown to you, they are as intrigued by you as you are by them.

But then you don't know what to say, you look at the cashier and get your carrier bag ready, and before you know it, you have gone your separate ways. That was it. A tragic missed opportunity.

Why are so many similar opportunities missed every day? In most cases there's one simple reason: fear. Fear of looking a fool, being embarrassed or how you fear you would feel if you were rejected. So we do the rejection for them. The only way you'll ever find out what someone has put into their shopping cart (as above), is to talk to them. Personally I blame our mothers. What did they tell us over and over again when we were children? *"Don't talk to strangers!"* So, most of the time, we don't. Maybe we learned that lesson a bit too well.

Obviously I'm not suggesting you put yourself at physical risk. You're not going to go up to a stranger in a dark alleyway, late at night to say *"Hi"*. At least I hope you won't.

All too often we talk ourselves out of initiating even a friendly conversation because we turn it into a much bigger deal than it is. We attach far too much meaning to a situation and by focusing so much on our own fears about what other people may think about us, we paralyse ourselves into doing nothing.

> TIP: If you see someone who interests you for whatever reason, just say *"Hi"*, smile warmly and give some sort of low-key compliment. Maybe: *"You look happy/great/full of beans today."* At least it makes the person feel good. Even if they don't choose to continue the conversation, you haven't lost anything. But they've gained something. And it costs you nothing.

Shyness inhibits behaviour, closing down possible options. Extreme shyness can have a crippling effect on somoeone's life. The root of all shyness is invariably linked to low self-esteem, a lack of self-confidence and chronic over-analysis of a situation. In simple terms, extreme shyness is actually being so wrapped up in yourself, you convince yourself that everyone else cares as much about what you think and feel, as you do. They don't. Despite that, some people are so inner-directed they can talk themselves out of even saying *"Hello"* in a nanosecond!

Imagine for a moment how liberating it could be for you if you had none of these fears. Talking to people (men or women) simply didn't bother you anymore. You accept each situation exactly for what it is, rather than allowing yourself to imagine a potentially unpleasant outcome.

Women in particular, are constantly advised not to make the first move. They argue: *"If the guy can't even do that, he's obviously a loser."* Well all I have to say on that is - what utter rubbish. Shyness can be a very appealing quality. Especially when you compare it with the alternative: a brash, over-confident chat-up line by a guy who is just looking for his next conquest. As a woman, who would you really prefer?

Shy men or women are absolutely not 'losers'. It's a label that's intensely judgemental, critical and disrespectful. Doesn't it say far more about the person who would use that word to describe someone else?

For many years I have been telling tens of thousands of business people at my lectures a simple truth. It's as relevant in a social setting as it is in a business one. And it's true everywhere, in every country I have ever visited. It's this: almost everybody feels anxious or uncomfortable walking into any room where there will be people they don't know. If that's you, you are normal. You are in the majority, not the minority.

So the next time you're at a party, look around the room and remember that regardless of how people look, almost everybody feels exactly the same way you do. When you know this, there's a simple technique you can use to eliminate any nervousness you might have. All you do is take the initiative to help other people feel more comfortable and at ease about being there. This is so powerful. You're helping someone else and simultaneously, by shifting your focus on to the needs of another, your own negative feelings evaporate. You simply forget to be nervous.

A lot of men and women have told me that this one technique has improved their lives forever. If you're a woman, give it a go. Practise on other women first if you have to. As your confidence grows, and your fears recede, initiate more friendly interactions with men.

If you're a man, give it a go, too. Regardless of how you feel, remember that a lot of women feel so constrained by the unofficial rules of social engagement. They are waiting for nice people to just say *"Hello"*. You're only being friendly. Some women may not respond positively – let it be their problem. It says nothing about you. Remember, you are **only** being friendly.

All this talk about how fear stops us from opening up new options in our lives brings us back to your imaginary shopping trip.

Step 3

You've rated yourself. But how would The One rate you on the qualities you believe are so important in others? To give you a more accurate answer, your friends (and current partner, if you have one) are going to help you by rating you too. I have to tell you that my team of male and female volunteers loved the idea of getting friends to do this for them, but getting them to pluck up the courage to do so was a different matter.

Even people I thought were fairly confident really struggled with the prospect of hearing the naked truth. They were so worried that they'd hear bad things about themselves. It was fear that was holding them back.

With a bit of coaxing and coaching, they accepted that the worst that could possibly happen was learning something new they could adopt to help make themselves more appealing as a person. The alternative was not knowing and continuing to meet a stream of new people in the months and years to come, never realising that they were being perceived in ways that weren't doing them any favours.

Feedback from friends who know you well and who genuinely care about you can be incredibly helpful. All you have to do is what Susan Jeffers says in the title of her bestselling book *Feel the Fear and Do it Anyway*.

So, invite your most trusted friends to fill in this questionnaire about you. It's available as a free download from the website that accompanies this book. Download it yourself and forward it to them, or ask them to visit www.BeTheOneBook.com/Q21. There's no registration or sign up. All they do is click on the link to open it up. It can then be printed out.

Ask them to put your name at the top. They don't have to add their own name if they don't want to. Tell each of these friends how important it is to you that they answer the questionnaire honestly. IMPORTANT: Don't tell them how you rated yourself.

Alternatively, you could just get a few friends together, open a bottle of wine and have a long chat about it. Be prepared for some lively debate. Your perceptions and theirs won't necessarily match up. However, this exercise can be life-changing. It is so worth the time and energy.

Step 4

When you've received a number of the questionnaires from your friends, your next task is to go through their answers and compare how you rated yourself against the way others rated you.

Identifying the **differences** between how you rate yourself and the way others perceive you is the entire point of the exercise. If you find there are large and consistent differences, you probably want to look more closely at those qualities and if appropriate, work on improving them. Consistent low scores in important areas might benefit from some attention too.

A final point on this exercise. Do not under any circumstances argue about the feedback (which will only teach your friends not to be honest with you in the future), or become defensive about anything you are told. The purpose of this exercise is to improve your self-awareness – it's not a weapon to be used against yourself. So devote at least some time to thinking about the similarities, too; what did they say that agrees with your self-perceptions? Perhaps you have now started to think of your current situation or your behaviour from a different perspective. With luck, you might question your existing priorities and be more open to different ways of thinking and behaving.

Invest some time thinking about what have been the most useful insights you've gained from this exercise? Write them down in the space provided on the next page.

Then put an appointment in your diary to assess your progress in three months and again in six months. If you decide to do something about these areas, you will almost certainly notice improvements. If you don't do anything, you won't improve. It is as simple as that.

By looking back, even over just a few months, you'll be able to see how much progress you have made.

What three areas are you going to focus on improving in the next three months?

1)

2)

3)

Additional Thoughts and Insights:

Chapter 3

From 'Me' to 'We'

So now you've laid the foundation for *Project You*, what are you going to build on it? Friendship, passion and commitment have been described as the three pillars of a solid, loving relationship. The solidity of those pillars depends on your foundation, or what I'm calling your Emotional Core, which we'll explore in greater detail in later chapters. Leaving your Emotional Core to develop by chance is a serious crime against a relationship. And in some cases it may lead to solitary confinement!

> *"Passion is the quickest to develop, and the quickest to fade. Intimacy develops more slowly, and commitment more gradually still."* Robert Sternberg (Psychologist)

Friendship

Let's look first at what true friendship is. I sincerely hope you have had, and still have some really great friends. These friendships are almost certainly based on a long history of shared experiences, some good, some not so good. You've laughed together. You've cried together. Over time, you have built deep levels of trust and respect for each other. From that friendship there is commitment between you. You would never dream of betraying the trust of a true friend. And they would never repeat anything you told them in confidence. You can say anything to each other without fear that you will be judged or treated harshly. You might not always agree with each other – but you'll be there for them during the tough times, as they have been for you in the past. They are prepared to listen. They always seem to know when you don't want their advice, just someone to talk to and be a shoulder to lean on.

Our true friends are the people we can call at any time of the day or night if we were to ever need urgent help. They'd be there for you. And you'd willingly do the same for them. How many friends do you have who would choose rather than feel obligated to do something like that for you? And how many of your friends would you be prepared to help out in exactly the same way?

Quite simply, that's what friends, and friendships are for.

Would you 'trick' or 'treat' a friend? True friends are treated. Well.

Now let me make a guess: you have never tricked, deceived or manipulated your true friends in order to get them to like you more, have you?

False friends somehow seem to have the knack of making others feel less good about themselves. They delight in setting people against each other, backbite, betray confidences and generally whinge and complain about the poor behaviour of others, never stopping to think that they are the ones who are being unfriendly and disrespectful. False friends sometimes equate feeling good about themselves by how bad they can make someone else feel.

How many friends do you have who are like this? Perhaps you've never even thought about it before. Now that it has been brought to your attention, how many of those you thought were true friends, are in fact false friends? Why would you (or anyone else) ever tolerate having a friend who makes you feel bad, or who isn't there for you or doesn't lift you up when you're down?

Let's be honest, sometimes we allow ourselves to have friends who do not have our best interests at heart. A lack of options may mislead us into believing that we need these friends. Especially when we feel afraid or lonely. By strengthening your Emotional Core, your 'need' for these false friends will diminish and new, more supportive people will come into your life. Friendships based on neediness or even desperation do not lead to long-term happiness. True friends enhance the lives of others. Period.

Perhaps sometime soon, some of your non-supportive friends can be let go. By surrounding yourself with people who appreciate your core qualities, you set in motion new opportunities to meet higher-calibre people. And one of those, just could be The One, for you.

> *"The only way to* ***have*** *a friend is to* ***be*** *one."*
> Ralph Waldo Emerson (19th century philosopher and poet)

Before that can happen you need to ensure that you are worthy of being the best possible friend to your existing friends. How might you be a better friend to them? The first part of your answer could be: *"By being a better friend to myself."* Think deeply about that question – and come up with some answers. Then practise being a better friend. Your true friends will appreciate you more. And you'll feel good about yourself by being a more proactive friend. If you're doing this already - great. If not, give it a go. Write down your thoughts here:

Now let's suppose you've met someone who has real potential to be a really good friend: same sex, different sex. It doesn't matter. You really like that person. How would you treat them?

Would you refuse to return their calls, make them do all the running or anything else you can dream up? Or would you try to give the false appearance that you're not that interested in them? Probably not.

Yet countless relationship books and magazine articles tell you to treat people who have the potential to be your best friend in ways that, quite frankly, you would only do to people you don't even like. There are so many rules, techniques, tactics and strategies to entrap or seduce a guy or a girl. Does entrapment sound like a good foundation for a long-term, successful and mutually happy relationship? It isn't.

Anybody, male or female, who is prepared to 'play' someone in order to manipulate them into liking them more is not being honest or even 'nice'. It's certainly not what friends do. This might not be a popular thing to state, but don't you know, deep down that this is the truth? Any friendship that doesn't start with respect and trust is far more likely to fail in the end. And if it takes a long time to fail, all that time is wasted.

I sense a loud chorus of *"Yes, but..."*

Of course, not everyone is honest. Many people have motives that are less than honourable. They will say or do whatever it takes to get what they think they want. Countless men and women routinely use their different charms to get whatever they want from what they think is a 'relationship'.

Playing games in an attempt to get someone to like or 'fancy' you can make things far more complicated than they are already. Putting extra effort into being spicy 'hot', whilst not wanting to be 'taken for a ride' is a classic example of this.

Inflame their desire. Feel desired. Give them what was on offer. That's all they wanted. They leave. You feel worse.

How many would recognise that pattern? If you do, and it isn't what you want, you need to break your existing patterns of behaviour by doing something different. But what, you might ask? If you aren't currently in a long-term relationship you might have found yourself thinking that you might never meet someone special? Or believe all the 'good' people are taken already. You might remind yourself constantly that time is moving on and that you're not getting any younger. Maybe you've convinced yourself that you're going to be 'on the shelf' sometime soon. Or anything else you can think about which feeds your fears.

But what if you had **no** fear? How might you behave differently? Really think about what it might be like to meet new potential partners without having any emotional fear. If you knew deep down that whatever happens, or doesn't happen, you have the emotional resources to handle it well. You are calm and curious. Interested and intrigued. How might that help you?

Without fears you would stop bothering to over-analyse the most trivial things your dates say or do. If you have to think about anything, doesn't it make more sense devoting that same attention and energy towards strengthening your Emotional Core as part of *Project You*?

What really attracts people to each other as friends, lovers and partners is their genuineness; their authenticity and a sense that they are comfortable in their own skin. A strong Emotional Core will help give you that; it may entirely dissolve or at least dilute your fears. Without emotional fear you will acquire a degree of quiet self-confidence. You'll be able to stop 'majoring on minor things'.

Play with This Idea

How do you currently protect yourself from getting hurt emotionally? And what unhelpful side effects have you noticed as a consequence of any defensiveness? In many cases this is perhaps the biggest obstacle people have to overcome.

1) As an experiment, for the next three months decide to behave in a warm, friendly way to everyone you meet or date. Take people as you find them. Do not judge or 'dismiss' anybody. And refuse to allow yourself to think 'What if' about anyone. Have no expectations whatsoever. This might feel difficult at first. Stick with it though. It gets easier.

You are simply warm and friendly. Authentic and honest. Regardless of whether you're a man or a woman, if you like someone, call them when you feel like it, not 'after a suitable delay'. Return the calls of those you like. Treat them as you would a true friend. Even if someone is not your 'type', or whether you fancy them or not, just be a friend. And no game playing.

You might be thinking: "but what if they take my friendship the wrong way?" No 'what ifs'. Let them deal with it. Just don't be cruel or deliberately misleading. Adopt a policy of 'open communication'. Stop trying to second guess anyone.

2) If you're confused about someone's behaviour or what they say – just ask for clarification, in a warm and friendly way.

3) After the three months are up, evaluate what you noticed about yourself and any new ways others responded to you. How easy was it? Did it help you relax? Is it something you would continue? I am confident you will choose to make this your 'new way'.

Personal Responsibility

Remember when you were a young teenager? For me, it was a very long time ago. Yet I still remember how so desperately I wanted to be 'grown up'. I thought I was. But now, looking back, I realise I wasn't. One day you reach the age when you no longer qualify for half-price entry or cheaper travel on trains and buses. How long did you cling on to the perks of being a child by trying to get away with paying lower fares, while convincing yourself that you were now a grown up?

Even though you may have wanted to be seen as a grown up, you could never be, until you accepted the full price of being a grown up – and that means choosing to pay full fare for everything. Living a First-Class life is always paying your share. To be

The One, you have to choose to pay full fare in life. Although that doesn't mean you have to refuse kindnesses from others: just never expect or demand 'freebies'.

Almost everything in this book is aimed equally at men and women. However, the above point refers specifically to some women. You can't ever be truly 'equal' if you insist on 'preferential equality'. Yes, of course it's nice to be treated occasionally. But not if it's a 'one way street' all the time. You don't expect your friends to pay for everything, so why discriminate against someone who could be The One by refusing to pay your fair share? That doesn't have to mean as much as 50%.

To 'be' equal, you have to 'do' equal.

And just to be fair on the sexual equality front, here is a light but firm slap across the back of the head to men. During months of discussions with women, the same complaint about men came up time and again: when a woman who has made some effort to look nice, far too many men 'just show up' as they are. They don't make any effort for the woman. A clean shirt and trousers would be a good start. Shaving would be better, dirty finger nails and dirty shoes definitely get noticed (and not positively). So guys, at least arrive clean. Women feel disrespected if a guy doesn't bother. She is also likely to conclude that if he can't or won't look after himself in even this basic way, what chance is there he'll ever look after her? And if this is him trying to 'impress' what is he like when he's 'off-duty'? He's dead in the water even before anything has started. And rightly so.

From 'Me me me' to Being Part of an 'Us'

This has to be stated: single men and single women can be quite selfish. The longer they have been single, the more selfish they tend to become. If you are looking for The One, be very conscious of the sources of all selfish behaviour, on their part and on yours. If you are selfish and not prepared to adjust your ways, you aren't being The One for the other person.

Selfish behaviour seems to have become an epidemic in modern society. Individualism certainly has its place but being The One is very different to 'looking out for number one'. Confirmed bachelors and spinsters (don't you just hate that 's' word?) spend the majority of their thinking time doing so about themselves. This can lead to a degree of 'self-focus' that has very undesirable effects within any meaningful relationship. Too much self-thinking can lead to an overdeveloped sense of self. We've all met people (men and women) who have developed the attitude: *"It's my way, or it's no way."* These inflexible individuals would probably benefit from being told occasionally: *"OK – get* ***on*** *your way!"*

We develop 'our own little ways'. How the toothpaste tube is squeezed. The layout of the cutlery drawer. How and where dirty laundry is kept. Loo seat up or down?

I heard this story about a woman who had been on her own for a long time and had become so house-proud she never invited a man back for coffee. This wasn't because she didn't like men, it was because she couldn't bear the thought of anyone messing up the cushions she kept so carefully arranged on her sofa! Think again of Sally in *When Harry Met Sally*: everything had to be 'just so' for her. When ordering her salad, it had to be served in a particular way. Or else.

And don't think it's only women. Tony wrote:

> *"My annoying habit is tidiness. I used to blame it on the military culture. My home has always been spotless and my whole life very organised. I have been described as the most organised straight man around! Other comments have included a very sharp "Have you got OCD (Obsessive Compulsive Disorder) or something?" I used to think that showing I can look after myself would be an attractive quality. But in reality it can be intimidating. One woman said so when we were breaking up after just two months together. Mind you she*

was the ex-wife of a genuine Hells Angel. Maybe it was because my bike is kept in the garage instead of the kitchen! Another female friend was going to rent my spare room but decided she would be too scared to upset things in the house. Things we may think of as 'endearing' qualities can have the opposite effect."

What peculiar little ways do you have that might irritate the hell out of other people? It doesn't necessarily make you a bad person, but always remember that anyone else with their own little ways isn't bad either. If you want someone to accept your weird and wonderful habits you have to be willing to accept theirs.

As obvious or as jokey as some of this may be, you would be amazed at how some people just can't or won't think outside their way of doing things. They really would prefer to be 'right' rather than 'happy'.

Selfishness in single people is quite understandable though. They enjoy massive independence and there's no one around to correct them. They can do what they want, when they want, where they want and with whomever they want. Yet freedom like this is so often taken for granted at the time. And is one of the first compromises one makes when entering into a long-term relationship. So, if you're single right now, make absolutely sure you: a) don't take your current independence for granted; and b) do all those things you've always dreamed of before you meet anyone. Do this with energy and enthusiasm. Now.

Get it out of your system. Because once you are with someone, you will have to compromise on at least some of those dreams. And if you ever become a parent, you will experience joy, as never before. But from the day your first child is born, your life will change dramatically, and forever. You won't want to swap it for anything, but independence will become a distant memory. So, if there's stuff you want to do or places to visit, get on with it.

If, in the meantime you do manage to meet The One while

you're enjoying yourself, as 'inconvenient' as this may be, simply adjust your plans. Or better still, do them together. The alternative of course is to sit and wait and wait and wait for someone else to give you permission to start your life. Which, frankly, is no alternative at all.

When two selfish people come together, tension and irritation are guaranteed. The more selfish or set in their ways they are, the worse it can be. And if one person is selfish and the other isn't, that can be even worse for the non-selfish one. Selfish people like (or insist on) getting their own way. If they can find someone who is prepared to let them get away with being inconsiderate, all the better for them. However, the victim is pretty much assured a miserable future. And the longer they accommodate the other person, the more quietly resentful they will become. At the same time, the other person will take their partner for granted more and more. Perversely, the more selfless you are with a selfish person the more contempt they may feel towards you.

In many cases, people don't even realise how selfish they are being. Then when the partner can't take their behaviour anymore, they wonder where the outrage came from and think that person is the crazy one. Perhaps they even end the relationship. The selfish one may not even realise why, and continue into their next relationship with exactly the same behaviour, oblivious to why they all keep failing.

People tend to continue being selfish the longer they get away with it. Ultra-selfish types even target genuine, generous and trusting individuals who end up as emotionally-involved slaves. Anyone who is used to getting their own way, or not pulling their own weight in a relationship, may enjoy an easy life. Today. But it probably won't last. The partner who is being disrespected or taken for granted will be storing up resentment and anger about their partner's laziness or inconsiderate habits. This can build for many years, until one day they snap or 'explode'. Because their partner has been so wrapped up in their own self-importance for so long, they often claim that everything came out of the blue. And sometimes claim they are the victim of an unreasonable, hot-headed, 'unhinged' individual. Marriage counsellors are then called in. Little or no communication over a long period led to this. Going to a marriage counsellor at this stage is often a complete waste of time. One of the parties has had enough.

To be The One, you simply cannot be a selfish person. But nor can you afford to allow yourself to become a doormat. Compromise and respect for each other has to be shared. And at all times, both parties need to remember that the benefits of being together must always outweigh the benefits of not being together.

So, be honest with yourself:

- How selfish or 'self-focused' are you right now, on a scale of 0-10? (If you don't care, go straight to being a 10!)
- In what areas of your life could you focus on, starting today, to become less selfish and less self-focused?

It's fundamental to any successful relationship that both parties transition from being a 'me' to becoming part of an 'us', whilst never losing one's sense of 'self'. You will always be a 'you' as well as part of an 'us'. And so will your partner. If you've ever been through the heartbreak of divorce, you'll know at first hand how the relationship disintegrates as one or both people return to a 'me' position. Selfishness kills relationships. Being consciously aware of how important this is, is essential if a relationship is to develop and become stronger. Even though all of this is about you, part of that includes preparing the ground for being part of an 'us'.

What simple improvements are you going to make to your behaviour based on the insights you have gained from this chapter? Write them down on the next page.

Personal Insights and Behaviour Changes

Chapter 4

Your Emotional Core

'Flatulence' probably isn't the first word you'd expect to see at the beginning of a chapter about emotions. But do you, without realising it, suffer from 'Emotional Flatulence'?

In the same way that certain foods lead inevitably to emissions of unwanted gas, are you constantly feeding your mind with so many unhelpful thoughts that it's only a matter of time before there's an inevitable and unwanted reaction: namely an 'emotional fart'? These recurring unhelpful thoughts ferment and stew inside, until one day they can't be contained any longer. You might lose your temper over something seemingly insignificant. Perhaps you speak harshly and later wish you could 'un-say' whatever you blurted out. But you can't.

In some cases, spending time with selfish and disrespectful people increases the likelihood of these sorts of reaction. For everyone involved.

Would you be prepared to accept that genuinely happy, calm and relaxed people don't suffer from these 'emotional farts'? They don't scream and shout or have tantrums. They're not 'difficult' or demanding. They don't whinge or complain. Why could that be?

Could it be that their emotional state is in complete

harmony with their surroundings? They tend to be emotionally stable and are quietly confident that they can cope with whatever life throws at them. They view life as it is, rather than being obsessed with the way it 'should' be. People with this type of emotional balance are highly appealing to others.

Daniel Goleman in his groundbreaking book *Emotional Intelligence* wrote: *"People with well-developed emotional skills are also more likely to be content and effective in their lives, mastering the habits of mind that foster their own productivity; people who cannot marshal some control over their emotional life fight inner battles that sabotage their ability for focused work and clear thought."*

But is it possible to adopt and absorb these qualities? Yes. Becoming more self-aware is the first step. Recognising the triggers that set you off is a valuable, long-lasting life skill. Learning how to deal with them is even more valuable. That is what the next chapters are all about. Together we will explore in detail the components of what I call your 'Emotional Core'.

Your Emotional Core

Our Physical Core is the collection of deep muscles inside and around the trunk and pelvis. This Core provides inner physical strength, protecting us from injury, and improves physical stability. Strengthening the Physical Core is a key objective in Pilates and Yoga.

In much the same way as your Physical Core protects and strengthens you physically, a strong Emotional Core can provide inner emotional strength and protection. Emotions can be so uplifting, yet the same power and intensity can cause untold pain and anguish, attacking our hearts and souls like a cancer.

The Emotional Core components are:

- Self-Esteem,
- Attitude,
- Happiness
- Kindness, combined with Compassion.

When you improve your self-esteem, you feel more at ease with who you are. By accepting yourself, you become less 'needy' of others. By moving from a low self-esteem to a healthy one, your self-confidence also improves. When you start exhibiting a natural sense of quiet self-confidence, you become more appealing to those around you.

Once you've improved your attitude towards yourself, this will improve the attitude you exhibit to those you live and work with. Other people will almost certainly respond to you more positively. This in turn contributes to your sense of well-being. It also reduces your stress, making you a calmer and more relaxed individual. This further increases the likelihood that even more people will respond better to you.

The combination of an improved attitude towards yourself and others, as well as improved self-esteem, increases the likelihood that you will start to feel happier in yourself. You can amplify this even further by adopting simple, yet effective happiness strategies, which again strengthen your entire Emotional Core. Each one feeds and nourishes the others.

Low self-esteem Healthy self-esteem Quiet self-confidence Happier Calm and relaxed

Unappealing Appealing

Poor attitude to self Poor attitude to others Respond positively Calm and relaxed

Talk to anyone who's had a personal tragedy and they will tell you that their lives were changed forever in just an instant. Accidents, illnesses and natural phenomena affect countless individuals every single day. Your Emotional Core is the best insurance you can have to cope with the effects of personal traumas.

The benefits to you and to everyone else you come into contact with have the potential to be monumental and long lasting. The more you attract other people, the more you will realise how the improvements you have made have had a direct contribution to the way others think of you. Your new found qualities will almost certainly encourage more of your friends and acquaintances to talk about you to others:

"There's this person who you need to meet. And they're single – at the moment!!"

Explode

Of course, we all have faults. Some minor, while others are far more serious and can have a hugely damaging effect on a relationship. An under-developed Emotional Core can be the trigger for turning minor faults into major ones.

An extreme example comes to mind. A very long time ago I was in a relationship with a woman who had been horrendously abused by her mother when she was a child, physically and sexually. She had never 'got around' to undergoing therapy to deal with her considerable childhood trauma. At that time, I had no idea that her behaviour in the relationship was as a result of that trauma. One minute she was loving, the next and for no apparent reason, she would 'flip' into an horrendous monster. She would scream and shout, issue threats to commit suicide if I didn't do whatever she wanted. She was completely out of control. I still remember being abroad on business trips and receiving calls at two or three o'clock in the morning. She was utterly distraught because I had 'abandoned' her. Yet I didn't abandon her until her totally unreasonable behaviour eventually pushed me away. I couldn't cope. Life had become a living hell for me too.

Ending that relationship provided one particular and highly relevant insight. One of her many outbursts included *"This ALWAYS happens."* She was completely unwilling to accept that the reason it always kept happening was that she was not prepared to undergo specialist therapy. I later discovered that she most likely had a condition called Borderline Personality Disorder. BPD, as it's also known, often manifests itself amongst those who have a history of being abused. It needs specialist professional treatment.

All of these issues only surfaced once the relationship had been established and she felt able to relax, and be herself. Everyone is on their best behaviour in the early stages of a meaningful 'courtship', but as it moves into being 'familiar', any issues someone has experienced in the past often return.

Their past hurt is passed on like a baton in a relay race to those who are innocent of any wrongdoing. Negative emotions, low self-esteem, insecurity, neediness, depression or unhappiness will leak out eventually. And these qualities routinely show up in the form of anger, distress, resentment, bitterness, extreme negativity and jealousy. In some cases their outbursts also include physical violence.

If you have experience of being in any type of abusive past relationship, it's essential you make peace with yourself and the perpetrators of any abuse before moving on to another relationship. If you don't, you run a high risk of bringing the scars of any past abusive relationship into the new one.

We all have our own ways of coping when we are stressed or upset. Taking it out on those closest to you is never going to make you more appealing to that person.

Implode

Then there are the men and women who have learned to contain their emotions. They've learned to deal with them by 'imploding'. This is a bit like a cartoon character that swallows a stick of dynamite. The dynamite goes off and blows up the character into the size of a large ball, before returning it to its original shape. They open their mouth and a small whiff of smoke completes the comedic effect. The only problem with this 'solution' in real life is that it never tackles the root cause of the suffering. And each time the person gets upset for whatever reason, the latest suffering gets added to their 'collection'.

The following provides another example of how someone with an underdeveloped Emotional Core might react to a situation in which they lacked sufficient information.

Unhelpful thoughts are described by the late Richard Carlson PhD in his book *Don't Sweat The Small Stuff* as 'snowball thinking'. A small snowball thought gathers more and more unhelpful snow, until it has grown to an enormous size. If you spend a lot of time on your own, thinking about yourself, your life, what you feel you deserve but are not getting, opportunities missed, regrets and unfulfilled dreams and desires, it's fairly likely that a small snowball thought will similarly gather size and importance. But only in your head.

An example of 'snowball thinking' might start along these lines. Your partner has said or done something that you don't understand. Nothing 'bad' as such. But you're a bit confused by it. So what do you do? You start thinking about it. In fact, you try to analyse it. Actually you do this over and over again. It starts to take over your thinking. This tiny snowball is starting to gain in size. Because you have now devoted so much time thinking about it, you have finally figured out what it 'really' meant. What was originally a theory has now been allowed to grow into something much more significant. Now you have convinced yourself that you 'know' what it meant. And it wasn't good. In fact, it is now proof that yet again someone has disrespected you. Or they have failed to live up to your expectations. How could they? What a bastard/ bitch! Friends then add fuel to the flames by agreeing with you in an effort to be supportive.

All the while of course, your partner is blissfully unaware of any wrong-doing. Why? Because there was no wrongdoing. But how do you think they'll get treated the next time you get together? 'Snowball thinking' has led to a massive case of 'Emotional Flatulence'!

Have you ever had any such experiences? Either as a victim or as the perpetrator? Almost certainly. We all have.

But here's the critical point: the above reaction had nothing to do with the partner's original behaviour. It was entirely down to the fact that the person with the 'snowball thinking' attached a series of incorrect meanings and assumptions to that innocent behaviour. This is the problem with over-analysis. As each wrong assumption was added into the mix, its destructive power grew. What needs to be recognised is how and why those assumptions came about in the first place.

Our past relationship experiences have created our life story. Unfortunately, in so many cases the story we tell ourselves is different from the actual reality. When we add together all the wrong assumptions, judgements, interpretations, distortions and filters we end up with a mishmash of half-truths, confusion, suffering and insecurities. And add to that the fact that single people in particular, by nature of the fact that they spend more time on their own, focus on themselves, and the 'reality' of their situation is often not real at all. It's a mental construction often built without planning permission and on decidedly shaky foundations. Many single people convince themselves that everything will be put right when Mr or Ms Right comes along. If only that was true. It's not.

What recurring thoughts do you tend to have that are not helping you lead a happier life?

1)
2)
3)

Imagine your life if you didn't spend so much of your time exhausting yourself by giving these unhelpful thoughts more attention than they deserve. It is possible to do this. And doing so will make you a far more appealing person – to yourself and to others.

A well-developed Emotional Core can and will protect you. It provides you with more emotional stability, flexibility and inner strength. When you know deep down that you have a stronger Emotional Core, those resources will help you cope with everything life throws at you.

The next chapter deals in depth with the first, and in some ways the pivotal, Emotional Core component – self-esteem.

For Readers Who Suffered Any Form of Childhood Abuse
To survive sustained childhood abuse such as neglect, cruelty, psychological and/or sexual abuse, victims develop coping strategies. They learn to shut out and bury their most traumatic experiences. These incidents get locked away, often for years into adulthood. Unfortunately, they have a habit of escaping and coming out into the open when least expected. Invariably this can happen when they find themselves in an intimate relationship. 'Holding it together' for all those years, they finally relax and it all comes out. Sometimes wreaking havoc with those around them.

If you were ever the victim of childhood abuse, but have never 'got around' to seeking professional help to deal with it, please do yourself the biggest favour of your adult life. Get help. Regardless of how well you think you're on top of it. Do it now. Don't talk yourself out of it. Get referred to a specialist. Now. Meet more than one therapist until you find someone you can really relate to. Choose one who is solution-focused, rather than one who only wants you to talk about the problems. Do all this before you meet a kind, loving person who you can share a happy life with. Be proactive – do it before you have to!

The long-term price of not addressing childhood trauma with the help of qualified professionals, and the effect it may have on a potentially outstanding relationship with The One cannot be overstated. These days, professionals know so much about the longer-term consequences of childhood abuse. Far more than you do. Your memories of those experiences are through a child's eyes. What happened to you is also based on the incomplete understanding of a child. Believing that you're strong enough to deal with it on your own may indeed be correct, but if you're not, you run the real risk of destroying your future happiness.

Just making the decision to seek professional help is in itself a transformational experience and will go a long way towards improving your self-esteem and adding massive strength to it. It could also be the kindest thing you ever do for yourself. And for The One you have yet to meet.

Chapter 5

Full Esteem Ahead

When I first trained as a hypnotherapist I was asked by Jennie, a good friend, to hypnotise her to lose weight. She was vivacious, voluptuous and appeared confident to anyone who didn't know her. I had the advantage of knowing her quite well. Before the hypnosis took place, I suggested she was carrying more weight than she would prefer as a way of protecting herself. I asked if it was possible that subconsciously, she thought it would make her life easier by keeping men away. This completely threw her. It had never occurred to her that this was what she was doing to herself. She readily accepted that it was probably true. In light of this, the hypnosis focused not on weight loss but confidence building. She went into trance quickly and deeply. The session went well.

A day later she went out and bought a new dress. It was tailored to her voluptuous shape. When she got it home, she took it in even further. That weekend she wore the dress to a party where she met a guy. And started dating for the first time in three years. Yes, the boost to her self-confidence had helped. But that isn't the end of the story.

A few months later I asked how things were going with her new boyfriend. Not too well. Jennie said that he only came round when he wanted to stay for 'benefits'. I asked: *"So what are you going to do about this?"* She answered: *"Oh, I suppose I'll wait for him to finish with me."*

It was a Thursday. I suggested she finish with him over the weekend and that I would call her on the Monday to hear what she had decided. Initially, she wasn't too happy about my suggestion, but quickly realised that she was repeating her past. She said she was going to end the relationship. On Monday, as promised, I rang to ask how things had gone. Yes, she had dumped him. I asked how she felt about it. She said it felt weird at first, because she had never done this before. And then added: *"I feel great. It's like a huge weight has been lifted off my shoulders."*

This was her therapy, not the hypnosis. Perhaps she had been right all along. She did want to lose weight: the emotional weight that had been dragging her down for years.

By ending the relationship with this inconsiderate man she asserted herself. For the first time, she realised that she didn't have to accept poor behaviour by others or wait to be dumped herself (and we all know the effect that has on one's feelings of self-worth). She could take the initiative and accept responsibility for herself from now on.

A low self-esteem and poor self-confidence were the root cause of all this. Yet she wasn't aware of it. She hadn't realised that her self-esteem and the relationship she had with herself was having such a powerful, and in this case, negative impact on her life.

How's your self-esteem and self-confidence right now? And how is it affecting the way you view yourself, how you interpret situations and the way people perceive you, especially among those you date?

Self-Esteem is the first of the four Emotional Core components. In this chapter we will explore what self-esteem is, how your past and current thinking patterns and behaviour influence your self-confidence. There are a number of questions and exercises. Please take some time to write down your answers. It is essential that you understand the level of your self-esteem, and the factors that have contributed to it so far in your life, before you can be more open to new and better options.

First the good news: weak, needy and inadequate 'victims' with little or no self-confidence and low self-esteem are in high demand these days.

Now the bad news: controlling bullies just love 'em.

And the more insecure and unloved anyone feels about themselves, the easier it is for the unscrupulous to entice them into a life of unrewarding servitude, keeping them under their control by dishing out daily doses of cruel put-downs, psychological and emotional, as well as physical, abuse. And each time they get away with it, it confirms in the mind of the victim that they 'deserve' such harsh treatment because they really are that inadequate. In many cases, those with chronically poor self-confidence sentence themselves to years of emotional torment and abuse because they are willing to settle for anyone who shows interest in them. The desperate need to feel wanted, even by a disgusting toerag, becomes a substitute for feeling loved. Those with low self-esteem are most likely to say, or at least to think: *"Who else would want me?"* In their minds at least, even settling for second best is too good for them. This becomes a vicious circle.

Anybody is NOT better than nobody.

So on a scale of 0-10, how high is your self-esteem and self-confidence right now?

0 1 2 3 4 5 6 7 8 9 10

Extremely low self-esteem can mean you always feel deeply unhappy and sense that you get walked over all the time, but you're not quite sure why. So less than a 5 is a sign that you would benefit from giving your self-esteem some much-needed attention.

Anything above a 5 is fairly healthy, although there's probably room for improvement. Is it possible to have self-esteem and self-confidence that's too high? Yes. Being 'egotesticle' (sic) or 'high-maintenance' will turn more people off you than will be attracted to you. Believing that you are 'worth it' or living a First-Class life is fine, but not if your partner is made to feel that they are Second-Class. Extreme selfishness or believing that the world revolves around you can make you deeply unappealing to others.

Aim for 'Goldilocks self-esteem': not too much, not too little, juuuuust right. Without a healthy self-esteem, emotional instability is practically guaranteed. That applies whether your self-esteem is too high, or too low.

Reservoir of Suffering

Each time someone calls us hurtful names, especially people who claim to love us (and even more so those we call ourselves!), the remarks flow into what I call our *Reservoir of Suffering*. At the bottom of this reservoir is our self-esteem. It just sits there minding its own business. But as each new 'hurt' gets poured on top, that self-esteem is crushed by the sheer weight and pressure bearing down on it. Much like a shipwreck at the bottom of the ocean, our self-esteem is confined to the depths of our despair. Our self-esteem is drowned by the combined effect of these slurs and put-downs.

Low self-esteem affects your relationship with others, your physical and mental health and your attitudes towards sex: turning some people off sex entirely or leading to a sex addiction in others. It can also lead to eating disorders as well as drug or alcohol abuse. Increased stress induces irritability, headaches and stomach aches, accompanied by a recurring sense of feeling overwhelmed. Constant tiredness and wanting to sleep or just to lie down during the day are all symptoms of stress. Sleep is an escape.

Low self-esteem can lead to a combination of other debilitating emotions and behaviours that make life even more miserable. But it can be improved if you decide to make it a personal priority. Let's see how, because the benefits can be life transforming.

Commercial divers lift precious artefacts from the depths of the sea to the surface by attaching buoyancy aids to help with the lifting. So it is with salvaging your own self-esteem: one of the most precious cargos you possess. It can take a while, and requires some effort on your part. Especially when you consider how many forces are at work to push it down again.

Propaganda experts know that the lies and distortions they spread become 'facts' if they get repeated often enough. But you can make this same process work for the good, too. Repetition is the key to improving your self-esteem. This is why making daily affirmations can be so effective. (For a sample list of affirmations and a selection of daily Stop and Start Reminders see the end of this and all remaining chapters.) Create an environment that nurtures you, and provides constant reinforcement by the constant repetition of empowering thoughts and beliefs. The more time you choose to invest in improving your self-esteem, the quicker and easier it will be to make and see long-term improvements. You really can do it.

Help from your friends will add even more oxygen to fuel your recovery and inflate those buoyancy bags to lift your self-esteem back to the surface. So, make a decision to adopt small improvements every day from now on. If your self-esteem has been eroded over a long period, it is almost certainly worth seeking professional help. Especially if you have experienced any forms of childhood abuse. (See the end of the previous chapter.)

Sadly, those who are in most need of expert help are the least motivated to do anything about it. They feel so bad about themselves, so depressed, so lacking in energy or so overwhelmed by a pervading feeling of hopelessness, that they cannot take the steps necessary to get help. They may even convince themselves that they don't deserve such help anyway.

Men especially, perceive asking for help as a sign of weakness: proof that they are indeed as pathetic as they have been told.

They have too many problems, not enough time, or not enough money to do this 'right now'. These are excuses of course, not reasons. Such feelings and patterns of thought are a recognised sign of someone who needs to find professional help.

Finding and staying with The One is so much easier when you have solid self-esteem. Yet social conditioning, expectations, and what you think you can and cannot do, all conspire to knock the wind out of your self-esteem sails. As this true story demonstrates.

"You can't do that!"

Attending a large conference in San Antonio, Texas I found myself talking to two women. When they heard that I speak about relationships they started telling me some intimate stuff. This happens all the time. Invariably I get nominated as an 'Honorary Girlie'. Penny told me she hadn't had sex for nearly three years, Renee the other woman had had celibacy thrust upon her for 18 months. Neither were happy with the situation. Penny went on; *"I workout and I'm not exactly ugly. But this is proving to be really bad for my self-confidence and self-esteem."*

They wanted my advice. I said: *"If you just want to get laid, this is what you do."* When I told them they both said: *"You just can't do that. That's terrible. It's ridiculous."* I replied: *"You are both intelligent, smart and modern women. You can do what I suggest."*

They weren't convinced.

All I suggested was when they met a guy who they particularly liked (preferably when stone-cold sober) all they needed to do was smile (perhaps in a cheeky or mischievous way) and say: *"You know, I'd really like to kiss you."* I went on to explain that it was completely within their power to decide how and where they were going to kiss him: on the forehead, the nose, the cheek or on the mouth. They really weren't convinced.

Fast forward two nights. It was 2 am.

We'd all enjoyed the conference's closing gala dinner. A black tie affair. An older woman I had known for years asked if I wouldn't mind walking her back to her hotel two or three blocks away as she was a little worried about the neighbourhood at that time of night. Being chivalrous, I agreed. And then it occurred to me that I would then have to walk back on my own through the same neighbourhood. At that point, Penny offered to come with us so we could both walk back together. On our return, she slipped her arm into mine as we sauntered along the famous *River Walk*. Then all of a sudden, she stopped walking. Because our arms were linked, I came face-to-face with her. And then it dawned on me: she was going to kiss me. Not good. But my over-inflated male ego was wrong. Instead, she said: *"I want to tell you something. I thought about what you said a few days ago. So last night I decided to give it a try. I ended up having sex for the first time in three years. I just want to say - thank you* ***so*** *much."* To this day that is the only time a woman has ever thanked me profusely for sex without me even being there.

He wasn't The One. Penny knew that. But in her case he was 'The One for that night'. I'm certainly not recommending this behaviour but if it catches on, and you are a guy who benefits from this form of female assertiveness - you owe me a beer!

Quite seriously though, Penny's self-esteem was given a huge boost that night because she discovered (or perhaps, rediscovered) she had far more influence and power over her own life than she thought. Would it help her find The One? Who knows? But it handed back self-confidence, which in turn will fundamentally change the way she perceives herself when she's dating. That has to be a good thing.

Your Inner Critic

Sadly, after years of being put down, or being made to feel bad about themselves, many people learn to put themselves down before anyone else can 'get in first'. By doing this, they are fooled into believing that they have insulated themselves from being hurt by others, but it's the equivalent of punching themselves in the face.

Often they've faced years and years of insults and put-downs from a parent, partner or spouse who despite this professes to love and care about them. If that's the case, what ever they say must be true, right? Wrong! However, our inner critic often agrees with these put-downs. Even though the basis for the put-downs is false, we often believe them.

We all have an 'inner voice'. This voice can be supportive or destructive. The inner voice of those with low self-esteem tends to become their most savage and vicious critic.

If you're thinking right now: *"I don't have an inner voice."* That was it!

Our inner voice could be encouraging, helpful and supportive. Yet all too often it's a savage inner critic. Think of this voice as a potential coach. If you were an international athlete, how well do you think you would perform if you were constantly told how incapable you were of winning any races, or improving on your previous 'personal best'? Who would want a coach like that? But it's surprising how many of us allow our inner voice to drag us down. Its motives are sometimes honourable. Unfortunately, it doesn't always do a great job. Well meaning it may be, but it can get a lot of things wrong about you.

For example, if your inner voice thinks you won't be able to achieve something, it may be negative in order to protect you from feeling so bad when (not if) you fail. The voice knows that if you don't try something, you cannot possibly succeed. Therefore, you don't try, you therefore fail to succeed and the voice proves that it was correct.

Whatever you do to rebuild your self-esteem, much of that effort will be wasted if you don't redefine the relationship you have with that inner voice. No matter what progress you make in other areas of your life, if your inner voice is highly critical, it will scupper most of your efforts, dragging your self-esteem back down to the bottom of your Reservoir of Suffering.

That voice has been with you for so long, you have probably never questioned the accuracy of anything it has said to you, or its motives. Your inner voice can be your own personal ambassador, but often it's an assassin.

What scripts has your inner voice used against you, perhaps for decades? Does it tell you what you aren't capable of? Why you don't deserve to be happy? How and why you are unworthy of anything better? Why you deserve any abuse you receive?

This inner voice routinely interprets a situation, or something someone says, and persuades you to respond in a particular way. How often does it express itself so forcibly that it sounds like it is stating facts about you when they are only opinions? How often have you challenged what it said to you? That voice has perfected the art of making everything sound so true and reasonable.

So how much does that voice run your life at the moment? Does it keep reminding you of everything you got wrong in the past? Your reactions may not be based on the reality of the situation. Your inner critic merely assigns a meaning to the situation that may or may not be correct. It could be based on wildly inaccurate assumptions. Sometimes your inner voice will even tell you what other people are thinking about you, but this voice does not have telepathic powers.

How to Take Control Back From Your Inner Critic

You must realise that your inner voice is yours, it belongs to you. It is not the full you, it is just a small part of you. You own it. This means you can control it. It is almost like having a pet; you can own a puppy but you have to take responsibility to train it not to pee on the floor or to bite visitors – or yourself. Use obedience training on your inner voice, too. It takes time, effort and energy, but oh how it pays off in the long term.

How might you behave differently if your critic was not trying so hard to control you? Remember that this voice is not you. It's someone who wants to control you. Give your inner critic a name. It doesn't have to be a flattering one. You can disagree with this voice. You can argue with it. Although it's probably not a good idea to do this out loud unless you know you are alone! Confront your critic. Prove your critic wrong. Ask or even tell your critic to shut up. When you hear negative comments from your critic, yell at it *"Delete, delete, delete."* or *"Shut up and get lost"*. *"You're poison. Go away."* Come up with your own comments if these aren't strong enough for you.

What if you could turn down the volume of your inner critic, or even switch it off entirely? Actually, you can. You own it, and you can do with it whatever you want. Do what you want, not what it wants.

Let's suppose, for example, you have learned to believe that you are stupid. How might you prove such an idea is totally incorrect? Let's do it now. For the purposes of this exercise, write down a list of situations or incidents where you have behaved in a way that demonstrates conclusively that you are not stupid. What good decisions have you made in the past? What good results have you created? What are your best achievements? You may find it difficult at first to come up with answers to these questions, but you have achieved a great deal in your life. Surrounded by negative comments from others and hearing your inner critic repeat such attacks, the truth about your achievements can be obscured. Universal put-downs that go unchallenged contribute to at least a dampening of an otherwise healthy self-esteem. When you hear your inner critic using words such as *"always"*, *"never"*, *"you should"*, *"you must"* – challenge it and demand proof that what it says is true. When you become more self-aware, you may discover that these words are used far too much.

In fact, remove the words *"should"* or *"must"* from your vocabulary. These are 'loaded' words and easily lead to feelings of shame, guilt and disapproval. Become more aware of others who accuse you of *"You always..."* or *"You never..."* They are trying to exert power over you. Don't let them. Increased awareness will help you question the motives of those around you.

In the same way that your critic has constantly and repeatedly put you down over the years, it's essential that you now learn a new habit of repeating healthy thoughts. You might think this is silly, but it really works. Notice more of your successes. Every time you do something right, quietly congratulate yourself. You're slowly starting the process of proving your inner critic wrong, and clearing space in your mind for a constructive coach to contribute to your long-term well-being. This will help you become even more appealing to other people.

Practical Ways to Boost Your Self-Esteem

When you improve your self-esteem, you increase your options. You will feel better about doing so, which in turn jacks your self-esteem up another notch.

From now on, make a decision not to allow your inner critic to say anything that undermines you. Ever. And stop letting your inner critic blame you for anything. It's probably wrong about you – yet again! It may take some time to retrain yourself and silence your inner critic but you can do it.

If others tend to put you down, decide to be more assertive with them too. Being assertive is about respecting yourself as much as respecting others. Aggressive behaviour is not to be confused with assertiveness. Aggressiveness is the equivalent of marching into somebody else's country. Assertiveness is standing your ground to ensure nobody marches into yours.

Learn to say *"no"* more often. Wean yourself off the notion that you have to say *"yes"*, when you would prefer to say *"no"*. The fear of disapproval often stops us. In reality, most people tend to think better of those with clear boundaries and who will not allow themselves to be taken advantage of. Someone who expects you always to say *"yes"* may be unhappy when you say *"no"*, but over the long term you may earn more respect from that person.

If someone puts you down, or makes jokes at your expense, politely say: *"Please stop doing that. I don't like it."* If they dismiss your request, repeat what you said calmly and politely. Or you could respond by saying something like: *"There are people who need to put down others to feel better about themselves. I hope you're feeling a bit better now. Pick on someone else next time."* If they insist on making fun of you for being *"so sensitive"*, respond by saying that perhaps they are the one who's being insensitive! Or simply get up and leave the room if you can. Just because you let people do this in the past, it doesn't mean they should be allowed to continue. It is better that they choose to think you have no sense of humour than to allow them to make you feel bad (or worse) about yourself. Just stop everybody from getting away with it. Do it calmly. There is no need to get irate or emotional about it. But learn to do it.

In general, stop letting others have what they want at your expense. Each time you allow this to happen, it chips away a little more of your self-esteem and reinforces any feelings of inferiority you might have. Stop making assumptions about what people think of you. You cannot read their minds, so don't be so sure they think poorly of you.

Identify the toxic people in your life: those who make you feel bad, deflated or worn out. Make a decision to minimise the time you spend with them. If you can't avoid at least some contact, make a concerted effort not to tell them about your plans and aspirations so they won't try to talk you out of pursuing what you want.

Who are the people that make you feel good about yourself? Invest more time with them instead.

Who do you perceive as the authority figures in your life? Parents are inevitably on the list. Gaining approval from these authority figures is usually important for most people, but there are some who are cruel and not supportive. If some of your authority figures have practically made a career out of putting you down, perhaps it's time to delete them from your list of people from whom you seek approval. After all, they've never done it before, so it's unlikely they will ever do so in the future.

Make a list of everything you like about yourself. Ask your friends what they think you're particularly good at. Write down everything. Ask only those you trust. Don't include individuals who have been responsible for putting you down in the past. List your achievements: everything from swimming a width of the pool to running a marathon. Also think of periods when you have felt really happy. List everything. Carry a note pad around with you for a while if it helps, so you can write down your past achievements as you think of them.

Here are some other things for you to think about. What is working in your life? What isn't working as well as you might like? What actions can you take to improve the areas that aren't working?

Do more of what actually makes you happy, as opposed to what you hope will make you happy. Decide to do something new every day. Adding together a lot of little things can lead to big improvements. Create a list of all the places you want to visit and all the things you've always wanted to do. From this constantly evolving list, find something each day to look forward to. Use your list to set yourself a new, personal 'enjoyment' goal every month: that's 12 new goals in a year. To make this happen, plan ahead more. Make appointments with yourself. And don't cancel on yourself. Your needs are at least as important as anyone else's.

Ask yourself questions like these:

- If I could do anything I wanted, and were guaranteed success, what would I do?
- What new skills could I acquire?
- What new hobby could I immerse myself in?

New activities can help you break out of the self-destructive thinking that often leads to harmful introspection. Worry and guilt have been described as the 'pointless emotions'.

There are some extremely high-performing individuals in the world. Invariably they are incredibly busy, yet they look after their physical well-being by investing time in themselves for exercise and relaxation. You can do the same, but only after you decide to make 'you' a priority. Make this part of *Project You*.

Invest time in making friends with yourself. Even though you may not feel like it, find ways to interact with other people. Make a decision to get out more. If you want help meeting people, you might want to get a copy of my pocket book *Meet, Greet and Prosper*. When you know the techniques for 'working a room' you could just learn that it's easier than you thought.

If and when someone gives you a compliment, have the grace to accept it. From now on, never invalidate a compliment by dismissing what they have said. It disrespects the giver of the compliment. Simply say: *"Thank you. That was a nice thing to say. I appreciate it."* Never say: *"Oh, it was nothing."*

Be more aware of what you allow into your head. Avoid harrowing movies, books and television programmes. Seek out uplifting entertainment.

> *"I will not let anyone walk through my mind with their dirty feet."* Mahatma Gandhi

Accept that you can change if you want to do so enough. All change can be uncomfortable or even frightening at first. Acting 'as if' you have confidence in whatever you do can be a major contributor towards actually being more confident. By making small changes and improvements, as your confidence grows you become more inclined to make even more changes and improvements. Slowly you will start to notice a change for the better in the way you feel about yourself. Sometimes we can't seem to help what we think about. Especially if or when we are in emotional pain. You may not realise this, but you can change your emotions. All it requires is making a choice. You can decide to feel something more empowering and more useful to you.

To illustrate this, do the following exercise. Sit or stand. Look down at the floor; make your shoulders rounded and take on the appearance of a depressed person. Now, without changing your physical posture, try to feel happy. You will probably find this difficult to achieve. Next, stand up straight; look up; breathe deeply. Then, again without changing your posture, try to feel depressed. It's difficult to do so. One of the simplest and most powerful ways to improve the way we feel is to simply stand up straight.

Maybe it's time to forget what has happened to you in the past. The entire world is open to you. You can do anything you want: if you want to do it enough. It's been said that life is lived looking through the windscreen, not the rear-view mirror.

We become what we think about the most. So, practise visualisation. See yourself being more confident and handling situations better. See those around you with happy smiling faces. Expect to be successful. This will improve the likelihood that you will follow through on your new behaviours. Experience feelings of quiet confidence and happiness. Practise your new behaviour with people who don't know you.

By adopting these behaviours and others listed in the Daily Stop and Start Reminders section that follows, you can only become a more attractive person: to yourself, to those you know already and to everyone you have yet to meet. Attractiveness is not the same as being beautiful or handsome. Those are genetic qualities. Attractiveness is an attitudinal quality that arises from healthy self-esteem and an appealing attitude to life. Everyone can be an attractive person.

Learn to accept that it is OK just to be you. Become the person you are meant to be.

On the next pages, and at the end of all of the remaining chapters, are long lists of behaviours you may choose to stop or start. Put a mark alongside only the behaviours you'd most like to improve. Then make a point of rereading these sections every day to remind yourself of what you have decided to focus on.

Daily Stop and Start Reminders

Stop

- ☐ Stop faking your self-esteem. Get real. Instead, learn to like yourself in a genuine way. Too many people confuse liking themselves with arrogance.
- ☐ Stop comparing yourself with anybody else. Especially don't compare anyone's looks, size or success. Ever. They are who they are, you are who you are. Nothing will ever change that.
- ☐ Stop letting others mistreat you in any way. Calmly ask them to stop behaving in ways that are upsetting to you. Don't tell them that they are upsetting you as this can give away your innate power. Focus on stopping their bad behaviour. If they refuse, just walk away.
- ☐ Stop mistreating yourself by being critical and judgemental.
- ☐ Stop taking your bad moods out on any innocent bystanders, especially those who are closest to you.
- ☐ Eliminate the following words from your vocabulary: *"should"*, *"shouldn't"*, *"must"*, *"mustn't"*, *"ought to"* and any other variations. Other words you might like to try reducing in your conversation are: *"I"*, *"me"*, *"my"* and *"mine"*.
- ☐ Stop taking daily setbacks too personally. Setbacks happen to everyone. Move on.
- ☐ How often do you try to feel good by making someone else feel bad? Stop this behaviour.
- ☐ Stop putting yourself down. Never do this ever again.
- ☐ Refuse point blank to be a victim for anything. Some like to claim victimhood as a way of getting others to give them attention or sympathy. It doesn't work. They rarely respect you and you feel bad. You lose on both accounts.

- ☐ For the same reason, stop telling anyone who will listen what's wrong with your life, why you feel so bad, tired or depressed. You're the one who will hear it over and over again. This will keep you feeling bad.
- ☐ Stop insisting that everything must be perfect. Life isn't.
- ☐ Stop saying *"yes"* when you'd prefer to say *"no"*. If you'd prefer to say *"no"*, say it. Do so, quietly and calmly. Don't explain why either. This often opens you up to a discussion about it, which could lead to you feeling the need to change your mind. It's likely you'll notice people appreciating you more when you are prepared to say *"no"* (without an 'attitude' though).
- ☐ Stop doing at least some of the stuff you do out of obligation. In many cases, those affected won't mind too much.
- ☐ And stop seeing people who put you down. That includes people you may currently think of as friends. Gradually phase them out of your life and replace them with positive, upbeat and kinder people.
- ☐ Cut back on watching or reading material that makes you feel bad. This includes too much news, too many beauty magazines or articles which seem to exist purely to criticise or mock others. Remember *"Garbage in, tends to stay in."*
- ☐ Stop worrying obsessively about what other people think. Why allow others to have that much power over you?
- ☐ Stop thinking about what hasn't worked out well in your life. The past is gone. Let it go.

Start

- ☐ Decide to make it a priority in your life to like yourself more. Notice more of what's good about yourself. Remind yourself of this as often as you can. Do it every day.
- ☐ Once you've mastered liking yourself move on to the advanced course: learn to *love* yourself! Not in a narcissistic way. Appreciate who you are at a deep level. You don't have to be perfect either. What matters are your positive intentions about life. You will never love or allow yourself to be loved by someone else if you can't love yourself.
- ☐ Copy the attitudes and actions of people with great self-esteem. Absorb those qualities. Make them real. Start with being in the driving seat of your life; being tolerant of others; being assertive; being open to better options; refusing to allow negative self-talk to infect your mind; learning from your mistakes without beating yourself up; not needing to play games or manipulate others; expecting positive outcomes yet refusing to feel crushed when they're not; ensuring disappointment is only ever a temporary visitor; having better things to do than being critical of yourself or others; being happy to listen and learn from others, and happy to 'go with the flow' without kicking up a fuss; devoting more energy to finding solutions than insisting that all problems are picked to pieces.
- ☐ Surrender to your low self-esteem feelings. Accept them for what they are. When you decide not to fight them, you are more likely to experience a sense of calm. And then you can change them.
- ☐ Accept yourself for who you are.
- ☐ Accept invitations. Just say "*Yes*". And then go.
- ☐ People with low self-esteem often neglect their appearance. So make a special effort to look after

yourself and your appearance. Even if you don't yet think you deserve it. New high-quality underwear, body lotions and perfume can have an uplifting effect. This applies even if you're a guy (well, make it cologne rather than perfume!).

- ☐ Trust your judgment a bit more.
- ☐ Take full responsibility for your current situation. Accept that you have what it takes to improve it, if it needs improving.
- ☐ Get enough sleep. You can't feel good about yourself if you're constantly exhausted, or relying on caffeine and other substances to keep you going.
- ☐ Treat yourself occasionally. Promise yourself a reward for a job well done. For any achievement.
- ☐ Each time you experience success of any type, remember to congratulate yourself – and remove any former habits you may have had to dismiss succes as *"nothing"* or *"just luck"*.
- ☐ Make a daily appointment with yourself (put it in your diary if necessary – and don't cancel) to remind yourself of what's good about you.
- ☐ Smile more. Do it with the eyes and not the teeth. Learn to smile to yourself too. When you are alone in the lift. Enjoy that inner glow. Do it for no apparent reason.
- ☐ Look at yourself in the mirror each morning for as long as it takes to see the unique and special you. You might feel a bit stupid doing this at first, but you'll get it eventually. You have permission to smile at the absurdity of it, too. Anything that helps you lighten up is a good thing.
- ☐ Do something every day, however small, to improve the important facets of your life.
- ☐ To help yourself, develop a new habit of helping others in small but significant ways. But don't overdo this by becoming a 'people pleaser' or a martyr!

- ☐ Thank people who give you compliments. Never dismiss kind words. It's disrespectful to yourself – and the person giving the compliment.
- ☐ Give more genuine and sincere compliments to others – and yourself. Notice the positive responses you get.
- ☐ Recognise the situations when you feel at your best. Where are you? Who are you with? Use this self-knowledge to help you.
- ☐ Do more of what you love. Find hobbies to learn new skills which engage and nourish you.
- ☐ Ask for what you want.
- ☐ Think more about what you're particularly good at.
- ☐ Notice and congratulate yourself more for what you do right. Treat mistakes as just learning experiences.
- ☐ Another way to feel better about yourself is to volunteer some of your time to a worthy cause.
- ☐ Forgive anyone who has hurt your feelings. If someone like Nelson Mandela can forgive his captors for imprisoning him for 27 years, what's stopping you from forgiving others? Let it go.
- ☐ Be somewhere quiet. Appreciate the calmness and serenity. Sit on a beach. Sit in the park. Walk in the woods. Go into the mountains and appreciate their grandeur and longevity.
- ☐ Look for beauty in all its forms: nature, architecture, art, people. Recognise the not-so-obvious forms of beauty. Make a point of appreciating it all.
- ☐ Exercise more. This can be just taking short walks, or a sport you used to like such as tennis or golf or yoga or even meditation.
- ☐ Create a list of what others like about you. Ask family, friends and colleagues. Reciprocate and tell each of them what you like about them too. Read your list regularly.

- ☐ Rebuild low self-esteem. Write a series of affirmations on little cards that you carry with you. Look at them every day to remind yourself that you're building a healthy self-esteem. You are well liked. Intelligent. Optimistic. Write down whatever you want, or aspire towards. Start each affirmation in the present tense, as if you've already achieved it, such as: *"I like myself", "I appreciate everything good about my life."* Adopt the most relevant affirmations from the samples on the next page.

Sample Daily Affirmations

- ☐ I like myself. I'm an OK person. I don't need to compare myself with anyone else to know this.
- ☐ I accept myself for who I am and who I have decided I want to become.
- ☐ I am enthusiastic and energetic.
- ☐ I have a great attitude towards life and to the people I meet.
- ☐ I know I have what it takes to be happy and successful in life.
- ☐ I am a more confident person.
- ☐ I have the capacity to love others and to be loved.
- ☐ I work hard when I am at work.
- ☐ I relax when I am not working.
- ☐ I respect my body and feed it with healthy foods and drink.
- ☐ I feel secure about myself and my future.
- ☐ I am confident that I can deal with everything that happens in my life.
- ☐ I remember to focus on what is working in my life and what I love about my life.
- ☐ Each day I remember to improve the lives of others, even if it's in a small way.

Add further personal affirmations in the space below.

Chapter 6

Attitude

"It's your attitude, not your aptitude that determines your altitude." Zig Ziglar (American motivational speaker)

Spotting a bad attitude is so easy, isn't it? Unfortunately, it's far more difficult to recognise a bad one if it's your own.

At the corporate conferences I facilitate, I have often asked audiences to call out the names of colleagues with the best 'can do' attitudes in their company. (No one is allowed to call out their own name.) What follows is always magical. Lots of names are called out. It miraculously and instantly generates a positive attitude amongst the audience. Some people call out the same names that have already been mentioned.

Occasionally I invite everyone who had their name called out to stand up to receive an enthusiastic round of applause from the rest of the audience. It's often quite emotional for everyone.

My next comment is designed to cut the atmosphere with a knife. I say: *"I wonder how many of you are thinking - why didn't anyone call out your name?"* I pause for a moment. Then I add: *"If we all met again in a year's time, what would you need to change or improve about your own attitude from today, for your colleagues to want to call out your name?"*

I go on: *"There are some people here right now who are saying to themselves – who is this jerk? What a waste of 'frigging' time... Guess what... I know who you are. It's quite easy for me to identify you. And I'm now going to say who you are... Ready? ... You've got your arms crossed."* You have never seen so many people unfold their arms so quickly!

I have received many emails from audience members over the years telling me that this five minute exercise actually changed their lives. For the first time, they realised that their own attitudes needed some serious adjusting. It had never even occurred to them before. As far as they were concerned it was always somebody else with the bad attitude.

How worthwhile could it be investing at least some time asking yourself how an attitude adjustment would be beneficial to you?

If, without much thought, you instantly tell yourself that there's absolutely nothing wrong with your attitude, that's a good clue that you really do need to look a bit more closely at it. Who do you know who goes through life insisting that they 'speak to the management?' Are you like that?

All too often a lack of self-confidence and low self-esteem will manifest itself in a poor or unhealthy attitude. This in turn will often create more feelings of low self-esteem and even less self-confidence, leading to a worse attitude. It's a circle of thinking, believing and behaviour that can ultimately poison you.

Your attitude is one of the first things other people always notice about you. A can-do attitude is your most valuable asset. It's free. And it's worth nurturing. It's been said that 'thought, attitude, behaviour and result' is an ever-increasing circle or outward spiral of impact. By improving what you think, you change your beliefs. Change your beliefs and you change your behaviour. Change your behaviour and you change the results in your life.

The price of a bad or unhealthy attitude can be huge. Not only to everyone else who comes into contact with you, but to you personally. A friend of mine told me this story. A particular guy always goes to see his son play football. Because he only ever talks about why his ex-wife was so horrible, the other dads wait to see which side of the pitch he goes to: they then go to the opposite one. When you allow your attitude to control you, rather than you controlling it, you become someone who is constantly reacting to your own emotions and moods and nothing else. In extreme cases, people will avoid you like the divorced dad just mentioned.

Recently I spoke at a singles event. I met a man who started most sentences with the words: *"I hate it when..."* At the same event a single woman kept using the word *"scary"* while she talked. What words do you tend to use a lot that could be giving you invaluable clues about your hidden attitude to life? Being aware of what you say, and how it relates to what you think deep down, can be an extremely helpful starting point for adjusting an existing unhelpful attitude.

For many, it has taken years of diligent effort for them to achieve world-class status as a negative thinker. If you can identify with this, cleansing yourself of negative thoughts is likely to take a while. Accept that it will. Before any improvements can take place, you have to start with the simple decision that having a positive attitude is something worth having and worth working towards.

Attitude is the second pillar of your Emotional Core.

Welcome to Wally World

In the lead up to one particular conference, I asked the CEO of a medium-sized company who he thought had the best attitude in the company. Without any hesitation he told me it was a particular cleaner in their workshop. I was impressed that the CEO would know someone in such a lowly position. And have such a high opinion of him too. The focus of this particular conference was about how the attitude of staff impacted external customers and their internal ones: their work colleagues.

The cleaner was too nervous about being interviewed on stage in front of his work colleagues, but he readily agreed to show me around where he worked and talk to me on video.

What a fantastic guy. Nearly at retirement age, he quite openly said that he'd never had much of an education but took great pride in whatever he did. When visitors came to look around the facility he felt it was important that everything was clean and tidy. I cheekily asked him if he was just *"sucking up to the managers."* He smiled and said: *"I'm from up North. Anybody who knows me, also knows that I don't suck up to anyone!"* He went on to say that he'd come up with an idea that would make the large yard outside the workshops tidier and safer. He then explained that 'management' had asked him to find the best supplier to provide the stacking system equipment they'd need. They gave him a budget. And access to a computer, which he didn't have a clue how to use. But he decided to learn. After doing his research online and getting various quotes, he settled on one supplier. His pride at being able to say that he also managed to come in way under budget, thus saving his company a few thousand pounds, was wonderful to see. He wasn't trying to be liked. It's just that he is.

We played the video at their staff conference. The applause he received when it ended was stunning. His name was Wally. So many of his colleagues told me afterwards: *"I want to be a Wally!"*

An improved attitude can have a massive and positive effect on how appealing you are to others. Maybe you'd like to learn to be a Wally too?

This next exercise will almost certainly offer you invaluable insights. Take your time interviewing yourself (or do it with a trusted friend) using these questions and add below any others you can come up with:

- What is your attitude right now? Why?
- How would you define your attitude towards life?
- How much does your attitude help or hinder you at the moment?
- How much are you a by-product of your moods, or is your mood what you decide it's going to be?
- What sort of people do you prefer to be with?

- What do you tend to do or say that might lead others to think that you have an unhealthy attitude at the moment?
- If someone accused you of being a 'toxic' person – what could they be basing it on?
- How committed are you to improving your attitude?
- Who are the people who affect you positively?
- Who are the people who affect you negatively?
- Who are the people you spend time with who drain you?
- Who are the people you spend time with who charge you up?
- How might you benefit if you avoided certain people?
- What would it take for you to become a 'tonic' person?
- What would you want people to say about you behind your back?
- What do you need to do differently so they would?
- How many decisions do you make each day? Would they be the same if you were in a good mood?
- What attitudes hold you back?
- Who is in your support team?
- What behaviours and attitudes in others will you refuse to accept in the future?

Let's be realistic here, very few people indeed are totally positive or totally negative all of the time. So learn to focus more of your attention on those with great attitudes. Who are the men and women you know who have one? I'd be prepared to bet that they attract other people like a magnet. They radiate optimism, energy, enthusiasm and vitality. Optimists tend to be happier, more successful and healthier individuals than those with negative attitudes. Spend more time with optimists. And make sure you are someone they would choose to spend time with.

Your attitude is linked to your energy level. You can quickly improve your attitude by increasing your energy. Enthusiasm increases energy. So learn to be more enthusiastic. Feeling tired? Ignore those feelings and just work through them. With some practice, you can nearly always work through it. Focus your attention on what's good about a situation and not what's wrong. Look forward to more things.

People with a great attitude are not 'Me Merchants' or 'I Specialists': people who constantly talk about themselves. Some do so because they are intensely arrogant and self-focused. However, others do it because they are incredibly shy and self-conscious. They believe they have a duty to keep a conversation flowing. And because they don't know what else to talk about, they stick with a topic they know intimately well. Themselves!

Either way, people who talk incessantly about themselves are far less appealing than those who don't.

> *"When you're wrapped up in yourself, you make a very small parcel."* Anonymous

If you tend to talk too much about yourself, and it's a personal habit you'd like to change, here's a simple way to do it. Every time you meet someone new, in any situation – professionally or personally, ask yourself this simple question: *"Does this person now know more about me, than I know about them?"* If you consistently find that they know far more about you, perhaps you need to: a) learn to shut up! and b) add the following words into your everyday vocabulary:

- *"Tell me more about yourself."*
- *"I'm interested. What do you think about....?"*

In fact, ask more questions. You'll learn a lot about people and it's perceived by others as polite and respectful. Because it is. Although don't turn your conversations into the *Spanish Inquisition* by bombarding people with a stream of interview style questions. Think of conversation as a ballroom dance: you both have to do the steps. And be careful not to step on your partner's toes.

This simple shift in conversation style can have a profound and positive impact on how others respond to you. And it's a fantastic initial step towards developing a more appealing attitude. In fact, if you want to take dating conversations to a whole new level, here is a tip:

The most successful daters know that the surest way to make a great impression is to help the other person feel better about themself. This isn't the same as laying on the 'snake-like charm'. It's about making sure the other person is validated, listened to, appreciated and respected. This means avoiding slipping into output mode, or becoming a chatter box.

In short, it's a question of working on being 'interested' rather than 'interesting'. Be more 'interested'. Genuinely and sincerely. And don't try too hard to be 'interesting'. Because what you will find is that the more 'interested' you are, the more 'interesting' you become. And it's a lot easier.

Doctor "No"

Who do you know whose first response to just about everything is a *"no"*? That seems to be their default setting. They suffer from what I call 'Knee-Jerk No Syndrome'. Rather than accept the views of others, they instantly want to challenge, actively seeking ways not to agree. Some are merely difficult, others are absolutely impossible to deal with. Some long-term single people become like this. A fine strategy if they want to remain single, but very bad news indeed if they want a loving, mutually respectful relationship. Invariably they are completely blind to this unhelpful and highly unappealing attitude. And for some, if it's pointed out to them, they'll instantly say, and possibly quite forcibly: *"NO. You're wrong."* But it's yet another *"no"*. By the way, when you hear people say *"Yes but..."* that also counts as *"no"*.

Do you say: *"Yes but . . ."* a lot? Try this simple change. Start saying: *"Yes and . . ."* instead. You will be amazed at the difference it makes in your conversations, and in the way others react to you.

Their negativity keeps people away because those they meet eventually conclude that life's too short to be cross-examined on everything they say or 'corrected' for most of what they do.

Some people can go to extraordinary lengths to justify why they feel the need to criticise, blame, correct, improve, point out, provide feedback and 'help'. They like to say it's because they 'care'. Who do you know who is quick to judge others yet refuses to question their own opinions and behaviours? Ask yourself how much you appreciate it when others do this to you. It's like pointing a finger at others when the rest of our other fingers are pointing back at ourselves. Try it now. Point at something and see where the rest of your fingers are pointing.

Medical professionals use 'ordinary' people as case studies all the time. So just for a change, let's take a doctor as a case study. I met her at a dinner party. She was 45, single, never been married, obviously intelligent, financially solvent, slim and attractive. On the face of it, a 'catch' for any man. And she was still looking for a long-term loving relationship. Her problem, as she was quick to point out was the 'fact' that the quality of available men was 'so poor'. She said that her friends couldn't understand why she hadn't found anyone. I was intrigued. Her conversation style was actually quite clinical. She also lacked warmth, her general demeanour was 'entertain me'. She was unwilling or unable to make any effort.

At one point she talked of a *"Repulsive man"* who came to her surgery wanting another supply of Viagra® in order to help him satisfy the **two** women in his life. She asked a colleague how it was that such a *"Repulsive man"* could have two women, when she couldn't find one man? Her colleagues' response comforted her: *"His standards are probably somewhat lower than yours."*

I just had to ask her a few more questions. Various symptoms were identified which confirmed my initial diagnosis:

a case of extreme judgmentitis. (You won't find this condition in any medical book – but I am sure you know plenty of people who suffer from it, and who cause others to suffer, too.) Was it a coincidence that she had chosen the medical profession? Perhaps not. She has a job where she is never 'wrong' about anything. Indeed, if challenged by anyone about anything, she can use the most effective 'get out of jail free' card there is: *"That's my clinical judgement."*

I couldn't help imagining that any man who ever dared argue with her would instantly be labelled as *"verbally abusive"*. If he ever tried to tell her something she didn't know, he would be labelled *"patronising"*. If she didn't get what she wanted, he would be *"inconsiderate"* or *"disrespectful"*. And if he showed sensitivity and consideration, he'd be a *"weak wimp"*.

Particularly intelligent and judgmental people, like her, also have the intellect and vocabulary to be able to rationalise just about anything they already believe. They can invariably 'prove' that others are always wrong. Such individuals have a phenomenal ability to protect their superior position. And will often go to extreme lengths to belittle those who might ever prove them wrong. These people are invariably toxic to those around them.

Toxic and Tonic Types

Toxic people demoralise, demotivate and force you to question your own abilities. Their pessimism can be highly contagious. They have a habit of expressing their opinions as if they are facts. And they will say or do just about anything if it helps them feel superior to you.

Avoid toxic people whenever you can.

Don't let them inside your head. Never ask them: *"What do you think?"* If you *have* to get feedback from such a person, rephrase your question as follows: *"How can this be improved?"* And gently insist they stick to answering that question. Needless to say, if you are the one who consistently demonstrates toxic behaviour, you will never be an appealing person until you eradicate such traits. That may sound harsh, but it is true. Those with unwanted toxic behaviour and the desire to improve will benefit even more from strengthening their Emotional Core.

Tonic people on the other hand understand the power of encouragement. They make people feel good about themselves.

Ask yourself: *"Who are the 'tonic' people and who are the 'toxic' people in my life?"* We all have them. Spend more time with the tonic people, and much less time with toxic types.

Family 'Shame'

As a teenager I was ashamed of my grandfather. At his funeral, I felt compelled to say so, too.

In my view, he was from the lowest possible class. He was a servant. For almost all of his working life he was a butler. Apparently he was a particularly good one. During the Second World War he was butler to Lord Montagu of Beaulieu, now famous as the home to the National Motor Museum. Later, he became a 'quintessential English butler' at the British Embassy in Washington, DC. Turn over the next page for a photograph of him. He's the one wearing a white jacket standing behind Sir Winston Churchill.

But what has this got to do with attitude? Everything. Let me explain.

One particular conversation I had with my grandfather completely changed my outlook on life and my attitude towards other people. I hope it gives you something to think about, too.

Like most teenagers I thought I knew everything. To give you a sense of how much I thought I knew, this was my version of 'polite conversation'. I told him how demeaning it must have been when he was a butler to wait on people all the time. He paused before saying: *"You know Roy, there are so many people in this world who don't know the difference between being servile and being 'of service'."* I had absolutely no idea what he was talking about.

He went on to explain calmly and patiently that being servile was indeed demeaning. It was lowering yourself, by slavishly doing what you were told by people who had little or no respect for you or other human beings.

In direct contrast, he believed being 'of service' was a deep honour and a privilege. To improve the quality of life for others was a sign of immense respect for that other person. He then explained that those he served treated him with equal respect. A deep level of trust was an essential ingredient of this. I honestly cannot recall any occasion when he said anything bad about anyone. Ever. I checked this with other members of my family. They all agreed.

I was asked to deliver the eulogy at his funeral. Below is part of what I said. It was probably the most challenging speech I have ever given. How do you summarise 99 years of someone's life in less than ten minutes?

When I speak to business audiences all over the world, I often ask the question: *"Do you brighten a room when you walk in – or when you leave?"* I went on to say:

> *"My grandfather definitely brightened a room whenever he walked in. He did it with such quiet dignity and a genuine warmth and respect for others. I never saw him lose his temper or even raise his voice.*
>
> *"Nor did he ever complain – the closest I got to hearing him complain was only a year or so ago when he said that he couldn't read so well any more. But then he added – 'I can't complain because at 98, my eyes have lasted far longer than they were ever designed for!'*
>
> *"He was also one of the most wonderfully discrete men I have ever met. When he could be persuaded to tell stories about when he was 'in-service', he would never say anything that could possibly identify the characters he was talking about. It's quite interesting that the news in the past few months has been full of stories of how butlers and domestic staff sell their salacious stories to the press. We all know such behaviour would have disgusted granddad because he was such an honourable man."*

I then went on to tell the packed congregation about the conversation I had had with him all those years before, and the profound and lasting impact it had on me. I closed by saying:

"To me – my granddad was a true gentleman... Granddad it has been a privilege and an honour to be of service to you today."

Copyright unknown but acknowledged.

In exactly the same way, I really hope this book will be of great service to you, too.

Everyone can have a positive attitude, whether they are 'of service' or accustomed to being served. And there is one simple rule that will help you demonstrate a positive attitude, and which others will notice. We all learned this in childhood, but it is amazing how easily some people forget it. It is known as the 'Golden Rule': *"Act towards others as you would like them to act towards you."* My grandfather treated everyone with respect, and he, in turn was treated the same way, by some particularly influential men and women. What about you? Would you be prepared to be of service to The One?

A Motivational Learner

At the beginning of this chapter there's a quote by the American motivational speaker Zig Ziglar. The term 'Motivational Speaker' is not always a compliment. Some who feel they know better take great delight in scoffing at *"happy talk"*. That said, Zig Zigler is an icon within the speaking industry. He's a speaker's speaker. Many dream of being as skillful as him one day. To the millions who have heard him speak over many decades, he has offered enormous encouragement and has had a massive and long-term positive impact. He has also created life-enhancing attitudinal and goal-setting programmes specifically for children. Take it from me, this guy is a master communicator. I don't know Zig personally.

Let me share this brief story to illustrate his outstanding attitude to life. A number of years ago I travelled to the United States to attend the annual convention for NSA (National Speakers Association). Thousands of professional speakers come together to learn from each other. Some of the biggest names in the industry pay quite a lot of money to be there. If you are one of the star names asked to address the audience, you don't get paid for it. Not only that, you still have to pay to attend the convention!

I attended a particular breakout session about how to collect and integrate your own funny, true-life stories into presentations that will entertain and educate.

I'd got there early and was sitting near the front. I listened and took copious notes. Sitting in the row directly behind me was Zig Ziglar. This legend of the speaking industry was there to learn. Despite his many decades of world-class experience, his mind was still open. This is the mark of someone with an outstanding attitude to life.

How open are you to developing an attitude that can and almost certainly would open you up to new and exciting possibilities? Or would that be a *"no"*?

I hope you can now start to see how a healthy self-esteem can set the stage for a brighter, more upbeat attitude towards yourself, your life and those you come into contact with. The combination of a healthy self-esteem and a positive attitude inevitably contributes to your own sense of happiness. The next two chapters look closely at your current happiness levels, your happiness mindset and the impact this has on all of your relationships: family, work, social and especially intimate relationships.

The next chapter is all about 'unhappiness'. If you tend to feel unhappy about your current situation, you could gain valuable and helpful insights from this chapter. If you are a genuinely happy person you might be tempted to skip it. Please don't. You'll discover how some deeply unhappy people latch on to happy people, and like leeches, suck out as much happiness as they can under the mistaken belief that the more they suck, the happier they will become.

Daily Stop and Start Reminders

Stop

- ☐ Think of people you know with a bad attitude. What do they actually do to express that attitude? How can you ensure that you don't do any of the same?
- ☐ Recognise the early signs of negative thoughts and replace them with more helpful, empowering thoughts.
- ☐ Cut back on mental stimulation late at night, it can make it more difficult for you to get to sleep.
- ☐ Remove your TV from the bedroom. Make it a place for rest and intimacy.
- ☐ Stop depriving yourself of sleep. It's a sure-fire way to make you irritable and short tempered. It kills a good attitude.
- ☐ Occasionally turn off the news and current affairs tap. Negativity in the news is rampant. Talk shows sometimes deliberately inflame fear and disagreement. Why not choose one day a week where you deliberately don't read, listen to or watch the news. Notice the positive effect it has on you.
- ☐ Stop trying to invite people to your own personal 'pity party', telling others what's wrong with your life or how tired and exhausted you feel. Half won't care. The other half could be pleased.
- ☐ Stop criticising, blaming, judging, giving unwanted or unasked- for feedback. When others do it to you, do you *really* like them for it? No. In that case, stop doing it yourself. And if you try to justify it by claiming it's just you being 'helpful', nobody wants that type of 'help'.
- ☐ Stop spending time with anyone who tries to do this to you.
- ☐ How often do you use other people as your 'audience'? Stop hogging conversations.

- ☐ Stop participating in office 'gripe sessions'. They don't change anything and they just make your attitude worse.
- ☐ Don't participate in any other negative conversations. Remember the maxim: *"If you haven't got anything good to say about somebody, say nothing."* Become known as somebody who only has kind words to say.

Start

- ☐ Assume full responsibility for your attitude: it's no one else's job.
- ☐ Remember every day that you can change and improve your attitude, if you want to do so enough.
- ☐ Devote at least some time every day helping to make other people feel good about themselves.
- ☐ Think of the needs of others more often and offer a helping hand and offer to be a shoulder to cry on.
- ☐ Start to monitor your thoughts. Become more aware of the times when you think negatively. Ask yourself how you could turn each negative thought into a more empowering positive one, e.g. *"If I go over and talk to her, she won't be interested."* Replace this with: *"I wonder how interested she could be..."*
- ☐ Spend more time with positive people – and contribute to that positivity.
- ☐ Copy the behaviours of the people you know who have the best attitudes.
- ☐ Focus more of your attention on what a better attitude would bring into your life.
- ☐ Each day remember to step back and look at yourself and assess your attitude at that specific moment. How aware are you of your attitude right now? It's a useful and valuable skill.
- ☐ You can decide and choose whether you want to focus on problems or solutions. Realise that if you're not part of a solution, you're often part of the problem.
- ☐ Keep in mind that learning to be more positive deep down will mean you suffer less stress. And this will give you more energy.
- ☐ What you eat and drink is directly related to your energy levels and mood. Eat badly, and you will feel sluggish. This affects how you think. How you think influences your mood and therefore your attitude.

Obvious when it's pointed out, but how often do we remind ourselves of this simple truth? Rarely. So eat less fat, hydrogenated oils, wheat, salt or sugar. Eat less processed, convenience or packaged foods. Eat less red meat. Eat more fish, chicken, fresh fruit and veg. Drink more water.

- ☐ Feed your mind with good stuff. And starve it of thoughts that are not helpful. Cut down on horror and extremely violent films. If you are convinced they have no harmful effect, ask yourself what it says about how you have become so emotionally desensitised?
- ☐ Instead, listen to uplifting music, watch feel-good movies and read quality literature. Fill your life with quality of all sorts. Cheaper options often cost far more.
- ☐ Identify the most supportive people in your life. And be supportive to them too.
- ☐ It's your choice: good mood or bad mood.
- ☐ Do something helpful for somebody else. Become a volunteer. Befriend an old person. Listen and learn from them.
- ☐ The simplest and quickest way to lift your mood is to do some physical exercise. When you least feel like doing it, just do something, even if it's a short brisk walk. I challenge you not to feel better about yourself. To get fit, embark on a programme combining aerobic, flexibility and strength training.
- ☐ Start noticing the good in people.
- ☐ Laugh more.
- ☐ Learn to stop taking yourself too seriously.
- ☐ Look forward to more things. Organise more activities.
- ☐ Reconnect with those best friends you never seem to get to see.
- ☐ Learn something new. Enrol on courses that interest you.

- ☐ Find more ways to be less stressed, calmer and at peace. This provides the optimum environment for you to have a more upbeat attitude.
- ☐ Make a point of being pleasant to more people. And do it every day. Make it a new habit.
- ☐ If you find yourself thinking fondly of someone you haven't spoken to in a while, don't keep it to yourself. Get in touch and tell them why you have done so.
- ☐ By doing more of these activities you won't need to pretend to be positive any more. You will be.

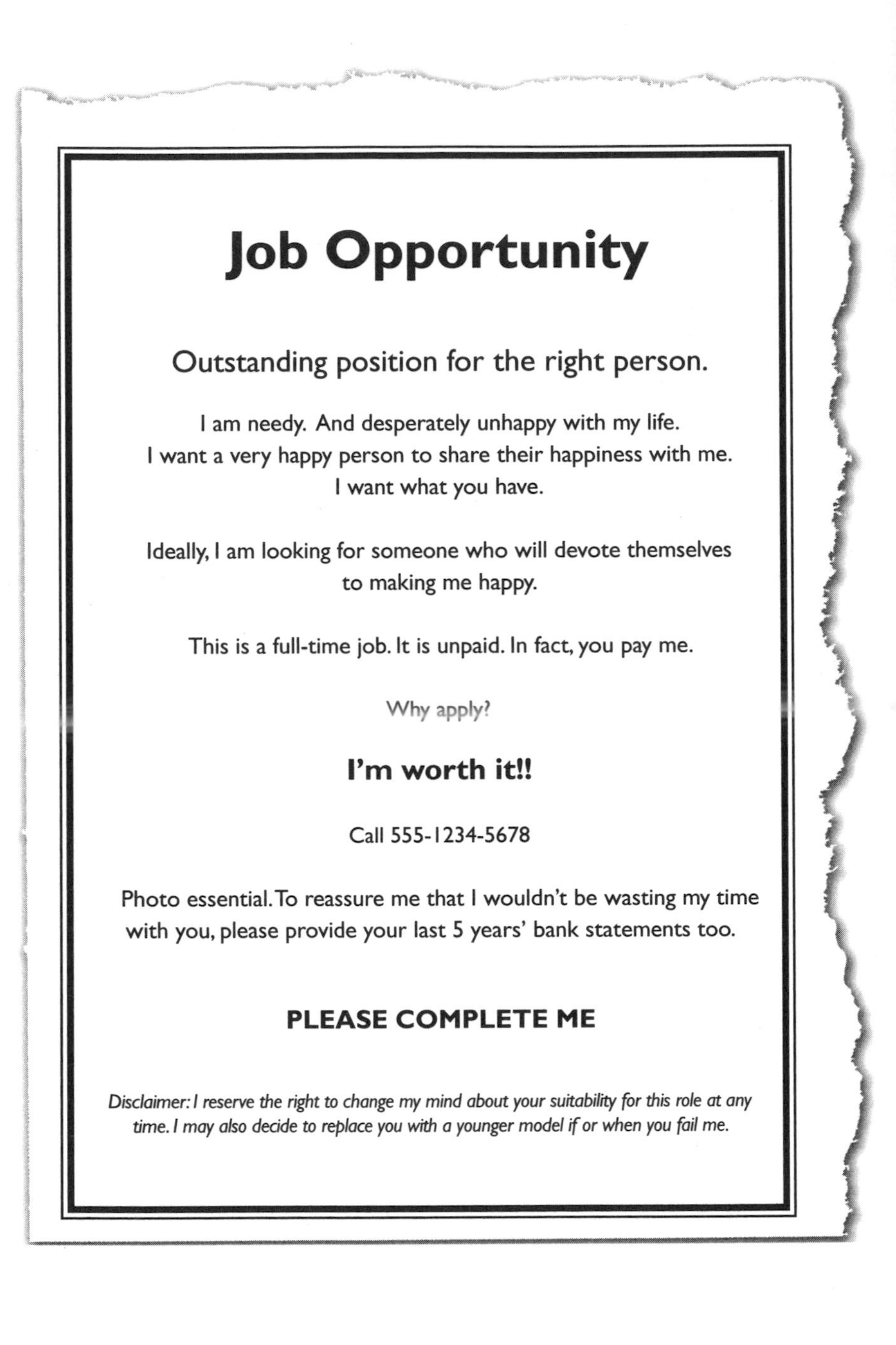
Job Opportunity
Outstanding position for the right person.
I am needy. And desperately unhappy with my life.
I want a very happy person to share their happiness with me.
I want what you have.
Ideally, I am looking for someone who will devote themselves to making me happy.
This is a full-time job. It is unpaid. In fact, you pay me.
Why apply?
I'm worth it!!
Call 555-1234-5678
Photo essential. To reassure me that I wouldn't be wasting my time with you, please provide your last 5 years' bank statements too.
PLEASE COMPLETE ME
Disclaimer: I reserve the right to change my mind about your suitability for this role at any time. I may also decide to replace you with a younger model if or when you fail me.

Chapter 7

Unhappiness Uncovered

What man or woman in their right mind would apply for the spoof advertisement on the previous page? You wouldn't, would you? That's precisely why deeply unhappy people don't ever advertise like this. It would put off far too many people. They attract partners in other, less honest ways.

The next two chapters explore the critically important happiness component of your Emotional Core. Chapter 8 focuses on 'happiness' itself while this chapter concentrates on unhappiness. Happy people are often targeted by the unhappy who believe they can suck happiness out of somebody else. And when it doesn't work (as it won't), things often get ugly for the victim who then also gets blamed for 'failing' to please.

It is simply impossible for someone who is deeply unhappy to be loving at the same time.

This chapter will also help unhappy people recognise the real root of their unhappiness, rather than what they may believe it to be at the moment. A happy person is always short-changed when they're in a relationship with someone who's unhappy. And an unhappy person misses out on the love they feel they deserve, but consistently eludes them. For unhappy people the ideas in this chapter can improve your life immediately. Thus helping everyone.

Knowing more about the various facets of unhappiness can provide incredibly useful insights into how you and potential partners experience the world. And the effect you have on others. This directly affects how appealing you are to a present or future partner. The nature of this topic might seem a bit 'down'; please ignore those feelings. This chapter is designed to help you.

What Unhappy People Do

I'm reminded of a chat I had with a single guy who claimed he wanted to be in a serious relationship. I started to ask him about happiness. A big mistake. He almost spat: *"I hate all that happy clappy crap."* I suspect if I'd been a woman he was interested in, he'd have hidden that. But it would come out sometime. Being that unhappy won't help his chances. When someone's default setting is 'unhappy' it will sabotage any present and future relationship.

The spoof advertisement at the beginning of this chapter provides a glimpse of how some people crave others to make them happy. They don't see being happy as their own responsibility. Someone else must make them 'whole'. *"You complete me."* was a great line from the movie *Jerry Maguire* but think about the idea behind it just for a moment. If someone else 'completes' you, it actually implies you were imperfect, lacking and incomplete in the first place.

When you have a healthy self-esteem and an appealing attitude you are already complete. Anyone in a deeply fulfilling relationship knows that their partner complements them, and they do the same. Each person adds something extra to the relationship. Being complete whilst in a relationship with someone who isn't, can be difficult and ultimately unfulfilling.

If you are happy, do not get trapped in a relationship with an unhappy person. Let me repeat this: avoid unhappy people.

Do not start or allow yourself to get sucked into an intimate relationship with one. Unhappy people may be appealing for short periods, but ultimately cannot be loving to others. They will want or even insist that they be showered with love and attention. In almost every case, the giver will fail to give 'enough'.

Therefore it is essential you learn to identify unhappy people accurately and quickly before you get saddled with the responsibility for 'curing' someone of their unhappiness. It's a lesson in futility. It can't be done. Here are some of the telltale signs:

- Oblivious to the feelings of others, they are only interested in themselves, their own thoughts and feelings.
- They have more rules than they know what to do with. And insist on imposing them on others.
- Constantly finding fault with everyone except themselves, they seek and demand perfection.
- They actively seek conflict to justify releasing suppressed anger or rage.
- They are always 'so busy', either to impress others with their own sense of importance or as a strategy to stop thinking about what isn't working in their life.
- They attempt to control the uncontrollable and demand certainty for everything.
- They obsessively compare themselves with others: especially 'beautiful people' from the media. They fail to realise that even celebrities themselves don't look as perfect as they do on the covers of magazines. Not only do they have the benefit of the best photographers, make-up artists, stylists and lighting technicians, once they have been captured on film a whole new set of skilled professionals use software to meticulously enhance them even further.

- They feel the world is against them. And things are harder than they need to be. They constantly play the role of a martyr.
- They are chronically fatigued on a regular basis, or want people to think they are, in order to reinforce their martyr status.
- They often 'hate' their job, feeling they are not paid enough, and expect or even demand to get back more than they are prepared to give.
- Money is a prime focus, although they often squander it whilst complaining that they never have enough.
- Keeping score with 'friends' is important. Who has more, who is winning, who is on top at any point in time.
- Afraid of being alone, they crave true intimacy and affection, yet push it away to protect themselves in case they get hurt.
- They keep moving the goalposts. Nothing you do for them is right. Even when you do what they tell you, it is never enough.
- If already in a relationship, they aren't interested in the well-being of their partner and don't care about his or her happiness, success, aspirations or comfort. It's always *"me, me, me"*.

These are just some of the ways an unhappy person behaves. Much of it is linked directly to low self-esteem. They figure, either consciously or unconsciously, that if they can force people into giving them more attention, it gives them power and will satisfy their self-esteem needs. It doesn't. In fact, it often feeds an unappealing attitude which drives high-calibre people away. The only ones willing to put up with this kind of behaviour are others with low self-esteem, who are prepared to accept this level of unreasonableness. To them, any relationship at all is better than no relationship.

Did you read through the list above and recognise elements

of yourself? If so, there is hope. You, in particular, can benefit from studying this chapter and applying many of the ideas you will find here. Adopting even some of these ideas will lead to many of these behaviours melting away. You can become happier. One of the ways is to realise that happy people don't make demands on others, nor on themselves. They accept things as they are, and find the courage to take action when improvements are necessary.

Even if you didn't recognise yourself in the list, everyone can benefit from ideas for greater happiness.

Assessing Your Current Happiness Level

1) How much do you want others to be happy? Shrugging your shoulders and not really caring is a good sign that you're not happy yourself.
2) What proportion of your thinking is devoted to what is wrong with your life?
3) What proportion is devoted to what is good or even fantastic about your life?
4) Does item 2 above get more attention than item 3?

On a scale of 0-10 how happy would you say you are 'most of the time'?

0 1 2 3 4 5 6 7 8 9 10

Where you place yourself on this scale is what psychologist Martin Seligman of the University of Pennsylvania describes as your 'set-point'. This set-point usually, but not always, remains fairly static through life. Generally speaking, whatever your set-point is today, it will be similar in 20 years time, too. That is, if you carry on with your life as it is today. This is key. Make a permanent change in your attitude towards life and you make a permanent change to your set-point as well.

We also have a set-point for our weight, which partially explains why dieters tend to regain their original weight when they go back to their previous ways. Permanent weight loss requires a permanent change of life-style: eating habits, exercise or both.

Anecdotally, I have asked many people of different ages where they would place their happiness level on this scale. The younger people I've asked seem to have an average set-point of 6-7, while older men and women in long-term happy marriages seem to have set-points of 8+. In many cases, people tell me that they had never really thought about how happy they were, even though most of us want to be happy. Knowing your happiness set-point can be useful, even if it reminds you that you're basically quite a happy person. If you're set-point is quite low, you can improve it if you decide to make a conscious effort to do so. The following ideas are simple to implement, cost nothing and the benefits can be immediate and long term. All you have to do is be open-minded enough to accept that this is actually possible and be sufficiently motivated to apply the ideas.

Having used these ideas in my own life, my set-point is now about 8 most of the time. Ten years ago it was quite a lot lower, in large part because of my unhelpful thinking patterns. It really can be improved. Like everyone else, my set-point fluctuates downwards and upwards on occasion. Ecstasy and joy sometimes visit, too.

For me, I'll experience a 10 simply sitting on the pebbles looking out to sea from Newgale beach in Pembrokeshire, west Wales, near where I grew up. Watching the summer sun go down over St David's Head is only marginally better than sitting in the same place during a raging storm in the middle of winter. It always reconnects me with life. No matter where I am in the world, I've learned to mentally transport myself to that place whenever I'm feeling a bit 'down' or overwhelmed.

You may also have such a place that makes you feel good. Call up such special places in your own mind to help improve your mood when you are down. Visualising like this is a form of 'resourcing', storing pools of positive feelings and retrieving them when you need them.

However, we get so sucked into coping with the day-to-day, we often forget to do what makes us feel happy inside and what is most important to us.

If you are unhappy about elements of your life right now, you are not alone, even though you may often think you are. In recent decades, general levels of happiness in developed countries have dropped noticeably. Unhappiness has therefore become far more widespread. And the number of people suffering from depression has soared. According to the World Health Organization more than 120 million people suffer from depression, which is of course an extreme form of unhappiness.

Depressed people find it particularly difficult to be loving, either to themselves or others. A single person wanting to be in a meaningful relationship whilst suffering from depression is a bad idea, especially for their future partner. If you suffer from depression I urge you to seek professional help before you enter a new relationship. It can truly make the difference between the success or failure of that relationship.

Sufferers already in a relationship put even the most devoted partners under intense stress. Alexandra Massey knows this at first hand. She is the acknowledged expert on depression from the sufferer's perspective. Her strategies have helped countless individuals to beat depression without resorting to medication. Author of *Beat Depression and Reclaim Your Life,* she talked to me about how the same strategies to beat depression can also be used to reduce feelings of unhappiness. She told me:

> *"Depression stunts your emotional growth. Learn to become more of a parent to yourself, replace every critical inner voice with nurturing, encouraging voices. One way of doing this is to get hold of a photograph of yourself as a child. Mentally step into the photograph and then, as an*

adult, sit down for a chat with that child. Ask the child what is troubling them. The child will almost certainly tell you. As an adult, you know how to sooth the child. Try it a few times. I can practically guarantee that you will feel different, and better about yourself within 15 minutes. I have seen it work time and again with almost miraculous results."

Mindset and Match

> *"A pessimist sees the difficulty in every opportunity; an optimist sees opportunity in every difficulty."* Sir Winston Churchill

Genuinely happy people think and behave in fundamentally different ways to those who are unhappy. There are countless people in dire poverty, enduring appalling living standards and some with horrendous physical handicaps who are far happier than those who appear (on the outside at least) to have everything they could possibly want from life. The way we think is the key.

A dear friend once told me how he often felt disappointed with himself and unhappy that he hadn't worked hard enough to achieve massive career success. He added that he hadn't really been that successful. I said: *"The next time you find yourself thinking in this way, take a very long, slow look at your son and daughter. Then ask yourself how successful you've been."*

He was stunned into silence for a moment. What followed was an overwhelming feeling of love for his children. As a truly devoted father, he'd allowed himself to forget about how much joy and happiness existed in his life already. This is just one poignant example of how we all at times think ourselves 'down'. Unhappy people tend to be brilliant at this. Happy people recognise when they start to think like this, and have strategies that replace unhelpful thoughts with more empowering ones. They usually do this without even realising it. It is second nature to them. It can become second nature to you, too.

Happy people tend to remember to be happy. They fully

appreciate what they have already. Unhappy people simply don't do that, they don't see any good in what they have, and they forget what being happy is. It's a learned behaviour. Ongoing feelings of unhappiness can be unlearned.

Invariably, unhappy people allow their unhelpful thinking patterns to focus repeatedly on what's wrong with their life. What's wrong with their job. What's wrong with their current partner. What's wrong with where they live. What's wrong with their body. They're too fat, too skinny, too tall, too short. Their nose is too pointed. Their boobs are too large or too small. Their penis is too small. Their fault lists are often very long indeed. On top of that they convince themselves *"I'll be happy just as soon as I get that promotion."* or *"I'll be happy just as soon as I save enough money for my dream house."*

Their lists go on and on. It's as if they they're going through life constantly chopping and changing their activities in much the same way as they would zap from TV channel to TV channel, vainly trying to find something interesting to watch. And even if they find something, they still keep zapping channels just in case something better crops up elsewhere. That is how they go through life: always on the lookout for something better. They don't know exactly what they want, just something 'better'.

The mistake they make is never questioning the real reasons for their unhappiness, which is the first step towards unlearning it. The true underlying cause of unhappiness is often related to the amount of time they allow themselves to think about what's wrong. They take their negative thoughts far too seriously. It never occurs to them that by thinking so much about what they've put on their fault lists they guarantee they will feel worse about themselves. Concentrating on what is bad never makes you feel better.

This was beautifully illustrated at a party I attended. I got chatting with a woman. She asked me what I did. The moment I told her, she opened the floodgates by telling me the intimate details of her life story: how her life was a *"car-wreck"*. (This was a phrase she repeated often.) How she *always* fell for the wrong men. How she'd undergone years of relationship therapy that hadn't improved her life at all. In fact, she concluded that she was possibly worse off now than she was when she started. It was obvious that she was a real expert on her problems. She had an incredible ability to articulate what was 'wrong' with her. She listed everything to me in great detail. I asked her: *"What strategies do you have to deal with your problems? What do you do to make yourself feel better about yourself?"* Her face went blank. *"What do you mean?"* she asked. I went on: *"What proportion of the considerable time you have spent with your therapist did you talk about how to feel better about yourself?" "We didn't,"* She replied. *"He just asked me about my problems."* The end result after many years of expensive therapy was that she had became a world-class expert at her problems, and was no closer to feeling better. How tragic.

Don't get me wrong, a good therapist can help patients in so many different ways, so what I'm about to say is not anti-therapy, or anti-therapist. Sadly, too many therapists focus on 'negative psychology'. They want clients to drag up all their past pain, often over and over again. They devote little time, if any, helping their patients feel better now. It's good for their business too, because clients keep coming back to them time and again for more 'problem' sessions.

If you are generally unhappy, you are probably already an expert on your problems. This expertise almost certainly won't help you feel better about yourself. And it stops you from becoming a more loving person, either to yourself or to a present or future partner.

- How often do you allow yourself to think unhelpful thoughts that deprive you of feeling happier right now?
- What are the most unhelpful thoughts you tend to repeat to yourself regularly?
  List them opposite:

1)
2)
3)
4)
5)

In so many cases, the root cause of a person's unhappiness is because reality refuses to conform to the carefully constructed fantasy that has been allowed to grow inside their mind. They keep feeding it with notions of the way things *should* be in their life. In many cases, their fantasy becomes their reality. And the deep unhappiness which pervades their entire life is in the gap between the real world and how they feel it should be.

This is a critically important point. Everybody does it at times. But unhappy people tend to allow it to dominate their thinking. And unhappy people are likely to withdraw from other people, spending a lot of time on their own, so they do a lot of this type of thinking. When you drill down a bit deeper into why men and women are so unhappy, it's often their habit of over-analysing situations, coupled with a desperate desire to somehow fit reality to the fantasy they've created in their mind. It keeps them unhappy.

You can devote the rest of your life to complaining about what your life should be. Or you can make a simple decision to make the most of what it is on a day-by-day basis right now.

Your life is what it is.
It is NOT the 'better' version you have created in your head.

Crucially, accepting this simple truth can have a massive and positive effect on your attitudes and behaviour towards other people. You are you. They are who they are. Trying to turn anyone else into your fantasy of what you have convinced yourself a partner should be will not only lead to huge disappointment (and the resentment that accompanies it), but it can make the other person's life unbearably, and unnecessarily difficult.

Remember to accept your reality every day.

When you learn to remind yourself daily that your life just is, over time you will learn to accept it as being OK. Some days it will be less OK and on other days, a lot better than OK.

Deciding to be Happy

Just suppose you could guarantee that you could change from being an unhappy person to a genuinely happy person in just eight hours. If it was guaranteed, how would you spend that time? Would you think about your problems even more? Or would you concentrate on adopting strategies that made you feel better straight away? Effective people devote a higher proportion of their available time focusing on solutions, not their problems.

> *"Resentment is like drinking poison and waiting for the other person to die."* Carrie Fisher (Actress)

In his work as a stress counsellor, best-selling author Richard Carlson PhD 'cured' countless unhappy people quickly, simply by helping them to adopt new thinking strategies. He often told his patients *"Being upset by your own thoughts is similar to writing yourself a nasty letter – and then being offended by that letter."*

How many people do you know who effectively do that every day of their lives? Each time this is allowed to happen they make it more and more difficult to be a loving person, and to fully enjoy a mutually loving relationship. It all starts with making a decision to be happy. This then becomes a priority in your life. You give it your attention every day. Carlson explained to his patients that how each of us feels, right now, in this moment, is a direct result of what we are thinking right now. Your thoughts create your emotions. They are linked directly. Unhappiness is an emotion, triggered by unhelpful thoughts. Without those thoughts, you cannot feel unhappy. Unhappiness simply cannot exist.

Thoughts are not real. They are part of your imagination. He compared dreaming, to the thoughts we have while we're awake. We know our dreams are not real, but we seem to want to believe that our thoughts while we're awake deserve to be taken more seriously. They don't. Just because you thought them, doesn't mean they are accurate or correct.

Carlson's 1993 book *Stop Thinking Start Living* can help you strengthen this area of your Emotional Core further.

Try this right now. Think about something mildly upsetting (nothing too serious). Relive the experience in your mind. You are now mildly upset. Your thoughts evoked those emotions. Now think of a time when you felt great. Relive that experience. Earlier I mentioned Newgale beach, my own favourite place. Recall your own deeply pleasant memory. Picture your scene, hear the sounds, remember how it made you feel. My guess is that you are now feeling better about yourself. Your thinking can help you be happier or it can make you feel unhappier. Adjust your thinking and you improve your life. Immediately. Even if nothing changes about your life externally. You do change it internally.

Unhelpful thoughts repeated over a long period have a devastating effect on anyone's well-being. And it's totally exhausting. So many suffer from perpetual self-critical patterns of thinking. These evoke deep and often painful emotions which trigger stomach-churning reactions. In many cases, creating a vicious emotional circle of pain and suffering. What we are unhappy about becomes what we think about the most.

Robert Holden PhD describes negative emotions such as guilt and anger as *guests* who often visit even though they have not been invited to come and stay. The same thoughts go round and round in your head, never getting resolved. Learn to recognise when unhelpful thoughts visit you, and invite them to leave. Mentally say: *"Oh, so it's you again. Please leave. I don't have time for you today."*

Meet the 'Hyper-Happys'

Pretending to be happy all the time won't make you happy. In fact, it could prolong your unhappiness. That's precisely what particularly unhappy people do.

Genuinely happy people are appealing to others. Unhappy people are less so. Extremely unhappy people know this and will often go to extraordinary lengths to fool themselves and others into believing they are happy. And in many cases it's because they so desperately want to appear appealing to others.

These really unhappy people can be spotted quite easily when you know what to look for. I call them *'Hyper-Happy'*. They have perfected the illusion of looking and behaving in ways that they believe represent happiness. It's usually too much. They are too 'up'. Too often. They don't seem to have down days. They are always wearing their 'happy face'. Sometimes it appears more as a grimace.

Party animals are an extreme example of the 'Hyper-Happy' type. Their obsessive, frenetic pursuit of pleasure, fuelled by large quantities of alcohol, illegal drugs, risky adrenaline-producing activities, and a one-night stand mentality, are in most cases a 'front' for deep unhappiness and inner turmoil. You will never meet a happy alcoholic who's still drinking, or a happy drug user. But they are so good at making you believe they are. They are hedonistic stimulation junkies. 'More' is never enough. Even so, they always focus on wanting 'more' now. Surely that would make them happy? More of the latest designer clothes, a better job, more money, a more loving partner, more children, more expensive holidays, a newer car; then they would be happy. But it doesn't work.

Think about it: truly happy people really don't need to get 'high' when they are high on life already.

Yet, to the uninitiated, Hyper-Happys can appear exciting, dangerous and intoxicatingly appealing. And anyone who's not as happy as they'd like to be is often attracted to these types in the mistaken belief that some of this exciting happiness will rub off on them. It doesn't. Hyper-Happys are so self-obsessed they constantly feed off others, who inevitably end up getting used, abused and discarded. Alternatively, once the Hyper-Happy has you hooked, they drop the pretence, reverting to their real behaviour: namely being unhappy. They were happy when they met you, but now they're not, so it must be your fault. And that blame is often sufficient justification to make their target's life a misery. They effectively say: *"I am not happy, you haven't made me happy. Therefore it is your fault I am not happy. And you are going to pay. I will then be happy."* It is flawed logic, but it's the best they've been able to figure out. After all, nothing else has worked.

You then try harder to please the Hyper-Happy, but nothing works. Which then makes you unhappier - and even less appealing to them.

Sometimes two Hyper-Happys get together. Both are fooled by the other's behaviour. And each one wants what they think the other person has for real. Both get disappointed eventually. Before then, the ride will often get intensely competitive, even dangerous, as each tries to 'out-happy' the other.

These unhappy Hyper-Happys are convinced that somebody else and 'better' circumstances will miraculously transform them into being happy, 'someday.' The trouble is the 'somebody else' always fails, the 'better circumstances' don't seem to arise (nor do they make any effort to improve their circumstances), and 'someday' never comes. It's more of a happiness mirage: always somewhere in the distance, out there on the horizon.

If you have a history falling for the wrong person, how often were you attracted to Hyper-Happy types? Or are they attracted to your real or pretend happiness? No matter: it usually ends in tears.

Truly happy people on the other hand, may look really boring by comparison. At least at first glance. Their happiness is inside. And it doesn't always show in the ways described above. We'll go into more detail about their behaviours and traits in the next chapter.

A Real Inspirational Hero

The closing speaker at a conference I moderated recently was one of the most inspirational human beings I have ever met: Chris Moon MBE. We first met on-stage at a conference over 10 years ago. I am proud to say that he has become a valued friend. Being blunt, by rights, Chris should be dead many times over. He was kidnapped twice in Cambodia by fearsome Khmer Rouge guerrillas. And survived. This is a rare occurrence. Most kidnap victims were murdered.

Then a few years later Chris was blown up. He stepped on a landmine in Mozambique, on a path that had supposedly been cleared of mines. His right leg was blown off above the knee and his right hand was so badly damaged from the blast that it had to be amputated when he finally reached hospital. Since then he has run many marathons and led various extreme expeditions in some fairly inhospitable places around the world.

Being blown up could have killed him instantly. His doctors agree that most people in a similar situation would have died. Not from the blast. But later from shock. That didn't happen to him because of the way Chris has conditioned himself to think. He has developed a remarkable ability to 'stay in the moment'. He absolutely refuses to allow his mind to run away with itself. When we let our minds 'run away' with themselves, we create those fantasy scenarios in our heads that are the cause of such widespread unhappiness. In Chris' case, his mental attitude literally saved his life on each of those occasions when he found himself in the wrong place at the wrong time. But as far as Chris is concerned, nothing was 'wrong'. It just 'was'. By accepting reality completely, he was able to remain ultra-calm and assess each situation accurately. He is absolutely convinced that everybody can do this. And he is passionate about helping people develop what he calls 'Personal Leadership': taking full responsibility for your life and making the most of what 'is'.

Doing this has the power to vastly reduce or even eliminate feelings of unhappiness. This in turn can open up whole new options in your life. And help you to become a far more appealing person to others.

Many years after his capture by the Khmer Rouge, Chris was the subject of a television documentary. He went back to Cambodia to retrace his steps. The production team managed to find the former Khmer Rouge commander who ignored (at great personal risk to himself) the order he had been given to execute Chris. In the film, Chris asked the commander why he had made the decision not to kill him? The commander said that Chris had no fear on his face, which could only have meant he was a good man. Because Chris was not thinking about what 'could' happen (being murdered) he did not look like a victim. Again it was Chris' mental attitude that saved his life. That commander could have made a very different decision, but he didn't.

As a trained criminologist, Chris is also passionate about why it is so important that we never ever take on the role of being a victim. As in the wild, you are either the predator or the prey. When you allow yourself to be a victim (as so many unhappy people do), you increase the likelihood that abusers (the predators) will decide to attack you for exhibiting prey behaviour. These attacks can be physical or emotional. A pattern of prey behaviour practically guarantees sustained unhappiness.

Read Chris' inspirational book *One Step Beyond* if you'd like to know more about what he's been through and how his mental attitude has helped him. And how it could help you. Ali, his wife has often joked: *"You don't need to read it though – just buy it!"* My recommendation: do both.

Daily Stop and Start Reminders

Stop

- ☐ Stop fantasising about what your life *should* be. It is what it is. And that's OK.
- ☐ Stop looking for happiness elsewhere. It's an utter waste of time. Your happiness is already inside you, all too often neglected while we chase around looking for 'better' happiness. For too many people, that real happiness spends most of its time deep inside us twiddling its thumbs waiting for us to simply remember that we have it already.
- ☐ Stop chasing a 'happiness mirage'. Appreciate here and now.
- ☐ Your happiness must never be reliant on somebody else.
- ☐ You become what you think. What unhelpful thoughts do you allow yourself to keep thinking about? Recognise the patterns of thinking you have which don't serve you well. Invite them to leave your life.
- ☐ Think less about your problems and more about feeling better.
- ☐ Stop comparing yourself with anyone else.
- ☐ Having or buying more will not make you happy. Pause more before you buy.
- ☐ Depriving others of their own happiness will never improve a relationship. Nor will it make you happy.
- ☐ Pretending to be happy or trying to be 'positive' can be a mere band-aid stuck on top of a deep sore. Such strategies don't resolve the underlying issues, they just cover them up.
- ☐ Stop trying to over-analyse the past. It's gone.
- ☐ Worrying is a wasted emotion.

- ☐ Continually striving for a permanent state of happiness is not only unrealistic but unattainable.
- ☐ Some people waste years whinging and complaining that the world is so unfair, rather than accepting it for what it is and putting that same time, energy and effort into making it better.
- ☐ Stop feeling lonely. Loneliness is actually not being happy in your own company.

Start

- ☐ Remember to accept your reality every day.
- ☐ Become aware of everything that isn't to your liking and just accept it for what it is. Notice how much stress seems to just evaporate.
- ☐ If you have a habit of putting other people first, all the time, think of yourself as another person.
- ☐ Look closely at the relationship you have with yourself. Improve that and you will miraculously transform your relationship with others.
- ☐ Pledge that from now on, you will never force anyone to behave in any particular way in order to make you happy.
- ☐ How could you become a better friend to yourself?
- ☐ Young children have the ability to become so engrossed in what they are doing that nothing else matters. We forget how to do this when we get older. Young children don't care too much if they are not experts at their play: it bothers us like mad! We take everything far too seriously. Our play becomes competitive, we need to be good, we need to win. This means it stops being play. Start playing.
- ☐ One of the biggest problems faced by unhappy people is their obsession with themselves. By shifting the focus of your activity and behaviour so that other people benefit, you create a virtuous circle where you benefit more.
- ☐ A good relationship adds to a happy life, it's not a substitute for an unhappy one.

Chapter 8

Happiness

"Happiness is when what you think, what you say and what you do are in harmony." Mahatma Gandhi

Years ago, Dawn, my personal assistant and I used to take it in turns to stand at the window and look up into the sky and ask the universe to provide us with whatever it was that we wanted that day. My girlfriend at the time would scoff at how silly we were being. We didn't mind because somehow it always seemed to work. One particular day, bookings for a seminar had been going slower than usual. So, it was my turn to stand at the window to ask the universe to send us loads of bookings. Five hours later, Dawn took a call from someone who booked nine places for the seminar. We duly thanked the universe.

Yet, my girlfriend didn't miss the opportunity to mock this 'co-incidence'. She didn't even change her mind when the phone rang again five minutes later. The same person asked whether it would be possible to add two more names to the nine people already booked. Did the universe really answer our prayer? I don't know. There is no evidence as such. But just because you can't measure something, it doesn't by definition mean that something doesn't exist. All it could mean is that we don't have an accurate tool for measuring it yet!

Not believing in the 'power of the universe' doesn't make you a bad person. However, being open or closed to the happiness that even 'coincidences' can bring possibilities can make a huge difference to the results you receive in life. I am convinced there's a direct link between this openness mindset and our levels of happiness.

Being close-minded is another example of the inwardly-turned thoughts that are the key to what makes unhappy people unhappy, as we saw in the last chapter. And it is another example of not living by the Golden Rule: before you dismiss what someone else says or does, think of how you would feel if they did the same to you.

Being open-minded is not the same as accepting everything someone else says. It means listening to them and respecting their opinion. You can still disagree, and can still try to explain why you feel the way you do. But with respect, not scorn.

How open-minded are you?

Happiness Heartbeat and Habits

We all have what I call a 'happiness heartbeat'. It's an 'upbeat' for happy types and a 'downbeat' for unhappy people.

During periods of great joy, the happiness heartbeat of happy folk may beat more quickly. At other times, a deep, calm contentment permeates throughout their entire body. They are at peace with life. The heartbeat is slow and regular . . . and still upbeat. It doesn't need feeding by external factors. In fact, genuinely happy people don't need loads of 'stuff' to make them happy. They are happy already. Because they understand what 'enough' means to them, they don't bother consuming or buying the latest fashions or unnecessary faddish toys. Able to delay gratification, they also benefit from the added advantage of enjoying everything twice: once while looking forward to it (which costs nothing), and again from the actual experience.

For so many other people, however, even though happiness is free, they insist on paying for it. Advertisers have perfected the art of making us feel bad about ourselves. They promise to make us feel better. So we buy their stuff, it works for a short time before its effects wear off. So it's off to the shops again for our next 'fix'. We even call it 'Retail Therapy'.

Happy people really don't need designer labels, the latest fashions, cool shades, the latest bags, gizmos or toys. They wear their clothes; their clothes don't wear them. Happy people are open to new experiences, new ideas and new people. How open are you to anything new? If not, why not? What if you decided to stop deciding why things are not a good idea? Say 'yes' to more opportunities, just for the hell of it. And just see what happens. (I'm not suggesting you do anything dangerous or reckless though.)

Above all, happy men and women know that happiness begins on the inside and radiates outwards. That's why they attract so much into their lives. Unhappy people believe fervently that happiness is outside, and must be given to them.

For happy people, looking after themselves is a priority. They know that food, exercise and getting enough sleep are critical to their sense of well-being. They make a personal commitment to do what it takes to be physically, mentally and emotionally fit. They schedule quality time to do this each and every week. They always have enough time to do what is important to them.

Genuinely happy people don't overeat and don't indulge excessively in illegal mood-altering drugs or alcohol. They don't need to. They know that fast food slows them down. So they avoid it. When they are feeling a bit 'down', they also know that the best way of getting themselves out of it is to do something – anything! They don't just sit around the house, moping. They act.

They know how to have real fun and are able to lose themselves in 'play'. It's part of looking after themselves. By ensuring they maintain a healthy work/life balance and manage their energy and stress levels, they don't burn themselves out. They know when to stop. They also know instinctively that being active makes them feel good, whether or not they are aware of the physiology of physical exercise. We feel better after exercise because it releases endorphins into our bloodstreams. These are natural chemicals that serve to make us feel good and positive.

Happy people are action-orientated. They know that even the most outstanding athletes don't win all of the time. By doing more, they inevitably end up getting more and better results. And they are able to set realistic goals and be happy with the results. Not all of these results will be outstanding, but they increase the likelihood that some will be.

With a youthful outlook on life, regardless of their true age, happy people manage to preserve their playfulness, joy and enthusiasm. They don't care if they're not 'good' or accomplished at what they enjoy. They like themselves and feel comfortable with the person they have become over the years.

They are open to the idea of seeing how something works out without requiring a guaranteed outcome from the very beginning. They blame no one and know they can achieve almost anything if they apply themselves to it. Even if they fail, they will have gained something in the attempt.

Happy people also laugh a lot. Often at the most ridiculous things. They see the absurdity in everything. And they are not afraid to look or act ridiculous themselves from time to time. They feel good about themselves, they are not too worried about what others think.

They have learned to enjoy the 'now'. Happiness is made up of lots of little moments. They don't expect to feel joy all the time. They go with the flow, accepting reality and life for what it is, not what it could or should be. They don't always need to be right, and willingly accept that they don't have a monopoly on all good ideas. They listen to the opinions and views of others without feeling threatened. They are also open to feedback, which they take without resorting to defensiveness.

They become what they do and what they think about. They have 'good intentions' in everything they do and wish harm on no one.

They always look for, and see, the good in others. Without

needing to keep score, favours are given freely with little or no expectation of 'repayment'. Happy people are always happy for other people's success, and are proactive about helping others to feel happy. That in itself makes them happier, too. They always seem to have time for others and actively collect friends and happy memories. They are generally relatively uncomplicated. What you see is what you get. They have no hidden agenda and don't feel the need to impose rules on anyone else. If they have to reprimand someone, they do it respectfully, kindly and in private.

They refuse to beat themselves up emotionally and just concentrate on being and doing the best they can. At the same time, they don't squander their own time with people who consistently drain them. They firmly but politely minimise their interactions with negative people. They have learned to protect themselves against toxic people and poisonous influences.

Generally, they feel good about themselves and who they are, regardless of what shape or size they may be. If that shape or size starts to bother them enough, they accept the responsibility to do something about it.

These are the people who love their jobs and would probably do it for free because they aren't driven by money. Even when they don't love their jobs, they accept their situation and do their best without complaint. Prepared to give more than they gain, they invariably find they receive more than they expect.

And when it comes to love, even though they may have been hurt in the past, they aren't afraid to love unconditionally. The potential gain is worth more to them than the possible pain.

For happy people, life is easier. Less stressful. They accept reality. They see the good in others. They're not overly suspicious, they don't make demands of others, they don't make mountains out of molehills. They don't major in minor things. Little things don't matter. It may have become a cliché, but they really do see the glass half full and not half empty. They don't feel the need to say bad things about anyone.

Every happy person I have ever met likes themselves and they have learned that when they feel good about themself, just about everything around them takes on a more pleasant appearance.

Everyone can make a decision to be happy right now – in this moment. So focus more on what makes you feel happier. Start by answering these questions:

- What is your own definition of happiness?
- Who are the happiest people you know?
- What is it they are happy about? Don't guess. Ask them.

Finish the end of this sentence: *"I am at my happiest when..."*

1)

2)

3)

4)

5)

If it helps, create a fuller list in a journal. In really simple terms, if you want to be happier, do a lot more of what you've read in this chapter and a lot less of what was described in the previous unhappiness chapter.

Daily Stop and Start Reminders

Stop

- ☐ Stop blaming others for what you think is making you unhappy.
- ☐ If you look for happiness, especially elsewhere, you won't find it. And the harder you try, the less likely you will be successful.
- ☐ Stop demanding more. Of anything. It does not make you happy. In fact, it's more likely to make you less happy.
- ☐ Stop giving your opinion without first thinking about how your words will affect the other person.
- ☐ Stop acting towards others in ways you wouldn't want them acting towards you.

Start

- ☐ Happiness is a choice, and is free to anyone who embraces it. So embrace it.
- ☐ Tell yourself every day: *"I am already happy, I just need to remember it more often."* Write it down on a card if necessary. Refer to it regularly.
- ☐ Catch yourself being aware of the moment and deciding to be happy right then.
- ☐ Make it a daily priority to do at least three things that help you to look after yourself.
- ☐ Find something to feel good about today and every day.
- ☐ Play with what ever you learn. Treat it as a friend.
- ☐ Think more about what you have. Appreciate that, rather than wishing for something else.
- ☐ Write down every incident you can recall when you were at your happiest. Little moments. People, places. Write down what it is about them that made you feel that way. Make the decision to create more of those situations in your life.
- ☐ Take responsibility for looking after something, however small: a project, a pet, a person or even a plant. It moves your focus outside of yourself.
- ☐ Find even more ways to enjoy your life from today. When you meet a new partner they will then be encountering an active, genuinely happy person.
- ☐ Take responsibility for creating the calm, harmonious and relaxing environment in which you live. Whether you are living on your own or not.
- ☐ Spend less than you earn.
- ☐ Save 10-15 % of everything you ever earn.
- ☐ Find more to laugh about.
- ☐ Find something new to like about yourself every day.
- ☐ Get into the habit of picturing yourself as a happy, contented person. Regardless of whether you

are in a relationship or not. Remember, a partner complements you, they don't complete you.
- ☐ Happy people recognise 'enough'. Enough is their friend. They don't always need 'more'.
- ☐ Learn to expect positive outcomes.
- ☐ Accept any negative outcomes, and when they occur remind yourself that you have had plenty of positive ones, and that you will again.
- ☐ Decide to be happy today. Regardless of what happens. Or doesn't happen.
- ☐ Start your day by putting your left foot onto the floor and say the word *"thank"*, then put your right foot on the floor and say *"you"*. I challenge you not to feel stupid. At first. It might even bring a smile to your face. Which is not a bad way to start every day.
- ☐ John Gray author of *Men are from Mars, Women are from Venus* advocates what he calls the 90:10 principle. We are all responsible for 90% of our own happiness.
- ☐ Look for and find the good in yourself and others.
- ☐ Learn to become your best friend. Accept yourself.
- ☐ Be fully aware of 'now'. Stop and become aware of this right now while you are reading these words on this page. This moment is your life.
- ☐ Fill your life with life.
- ☐ Remember that happy people just are.
- ☐ Memorise the lyrics to the Monty Python song *Always Look on the Bright Side of Life*. Sing it regularly, with or without an audience. The rude version is more fun.

Chapter 9

Kindness & Compassion

On the back of this book, there's a short paragraph about my background and career. It says I'm a kind person. When asked to describe me, friends and colleagues chose this word above all others. I'm not emphasising this to 'big myself up' though. Rather, there is an interesting story associated with that one little word. An old friend was asked for her feedback after the cover had been produced. She wrote: *"Pleeeeeese don't use that word."* *"Why?"* I asked. *"Are you saying it's not true?" "No. Not at all. You are a very kind person – but it makes you sound so 'weak'."*

How interesting, I thought. So I followed it up by querying it with others. They also added that it can also make someone sound 'wet' or an over-eager-to-please 'lapdog'. (Which I'm not, by the way!)

So the question is - are kind people weak or strong?

Here are a few questions for you to think about. Suppose you are feeling really grumpy. How easy would it be to take out that grumpiness on any innocent bystander? Perhaps someone you claim to care about. By contrast, how strong would someone need to be in order to ensure that they didn't let their grumpiness infect that same innocent bystander? Being grumpy to people who are innocent is simply self-indulgent and disrespectful no matter how you try to justify it.

Practising kindness and compassion is far more difficult, especially if or when you are stressed, tired or irritable. It can require a lot of effort, commitment and self-discipline not to spread how bad you feel to those who don't deserve to suffer. It really is so much easier not to bother. Just bite off the head of anyone who comes within snarling distance of you. How appealing do you think this type of behaviour is? Do it regularly and you will lose friends. It's as simple as that.

Is your bad temper what you really want others to remember about you? Share only the good. Keep the bad to yourself. Better still, banish unhelpful and unkind behaviour entirely from your life.

In his book *Why Kindness is Good For You*, author David R Hamilton PhD, cites a study of 10,047 young people aged 20 to 25 from 33 different countries. The research found conclusively that kindness was more attractive than good looks or financial prospects. This applied to men and women.

In short, being kind makes you more appealing to others. The personal health and well-being benefits to yourself are also quite compelling, as we will discuss as part of this Emotional Core component.

What is Kindness?

The other three pillars of your Emotional Core, self-esteem, attitude and happiness, are mainly about what is inside you. Your attitude will, of course, have an impact on others, and your happiness may be contagious, but these effects are a by-product (albeit an important by-product) of your emotional fitness level.

Kindness, on the other hand is outer-directed. It's about others. It's the way you express your emotions to yourself and everyone you know and meet. It is a point of view that effectively says: *"This person exists. They deserve my attention, my respect and even my support."* Whoever they may be.

Who do you know who you would describe as kind? What do they do that makes you think that way about them? I'll bet it involves how they treat everyone they meet, not just those who are 'important'. The person who mistreats anyone is noticed, but certainly not positively. But a true act of kindness so often creates a deep connection with the recipient of that kindness. It means even more to the recipient when the giver has no personal agenda. They are just giving with no desire or expectation of anything in return from that person. Kind people benefit in other ways. So, how kind are you: to yourself and others?

You First

How much do you criticise yourself? How often do you tend to say negative things to yourself that you would never dare say to anyone else? Why do you do this? Putting yourself down is never kind to yourself, even if you've managed to fool yourself into believing it's a way of ensuring others don't think you have an overinflated ego. Attacking ourselves, before we give anybody else the chance to is a common behaviour amongst people who have yet to learn that being kind to yourself is an essential element of being kind to others. You are not more deserving of criticism than others.

**Before you can be kind to others,
you must be kind to yourself.**

Being kind to yourself is not just about the way you treat yourself emotionally. It is about being kind to yourself physically, as well. If you were a high-performance car, how well would you run on low-quality fuel? Pretty poorly. Stuffing our faces with junk food is not an act of kindness to ourselves. Too many late nights followed by early mornings may be great fun at times, yet an ongoing lack of sleep is not being kind to yourself, either. What about water? Are you well hydrated, most of the time? Or are your preferred liquids caffeine or alcohol based?

It's a cliché, but often those who truly value their health are those who have lost it. Looking after your physical body makes sense on a logical level – but why is it that so many of us have been conned into believing that the best way to have fun is to do harm to our bodies?

Millions run their most prized possessions, their bodies, on low-quality, although highly-convenient, rubbish. Fast food makes you slow. Poor quality food really does make you sluggish. What you eat and drink affects your mood and emotional well-being. Eat and drink crap and you'll feel like crap.

How often do you wake up feeling exhausted in the morning? How late do you go to bed? Our bodies require sleep. Living on just a few hours of it is not a sign of strength. Constant tiredness, even among the young, is now extremely common. It affects the speed and clarity of our thinking. And treating your physical body unkindly affects your moods, emotions and general sense of well-being. Everything is linked.

Now Others

Think about how all of this unkindness you are showing yourself affects you. How likely would it be that someone running their lives in this way would be capable of kindness and be compassionate to others? It's not that likely, is it?

Looking after yourself properly (which isn't the same as being narcissistically self-obsessed) actually increases the likelihood that you'll treat others with more kindness. Think of the people you know who are not kind. They are almost certainly self-obsessed, selfish and inner-directed, sometimes in the extreme, aren't they?

Why Bother?

Male or female, just about everyone craves intimacy, kindness and being cared for. *"We are actually genetically wired to be kind. This is why it is good for us. And it is also why, when we don't show kindness, or compassion, gratitude or forgiveness, it stresses our nervous systems and is not so good for our health."* writes kindness expert David R. Hamilton PhD.

Being kind to others makes us feel good too. It's a loop. The health benefits include alleviating the symptoms of depression, hurt, stress, anger and anxiety. Doing good, and being good also improve self-esteem. This is another example of how the components of our Emotional Core work together to nourish our overall well-being.

There is a clear link between how happy you are and how kind you behave. Happy people are nice to others, and being nice to others reinforces our happiness. There's that loop again.

A positive, caring attitude has also been found to lead to a longer life. Not only that, kindness is absolutely free. If you're prone to feeling a bit down or depressed occasionally, the most effective way to get you out of it, is to do something kind or helpful for somebody else. Without any expectation of anything in return. Doing so also gives you more energy which in turn helps you feel more optimistic. Our brain produces the hormones serotonin and dopamine when we are kind. These natural chemicals act on our brains by also improving our optimism. Optimism in turn tends to make us more generous – not necessarily with money, but generous with our time and energy. These are all qualities that make you more appealing to others.

By learning to be kinder and more gentle with yourself, you start to radiate those qualities to those around you. When you understand the bigger picture of kindness, it isn't about you, it's about helping others feel great about themselves. Which doesn't just help them, it lights you up inside, too. People pick this up about you, even if they are not consciously aware of it. The kindness feedback loop is very real and incredibily powerful.

Perhaps it's because random acts of kindness don't tend to make the news, so they stand out in real life. It's a sad reflection of our society's priorities that the more uplifting aspects of human behaviour invariably get pushed into the shadows by the news media, in favour of a constant stream of cruelty, brutality and inhumanity.

To 'be' special you have to 'do' special.

Acts of kindness get you noticed. In a good way. Ivan Misner PhD coined a widely known business saying which applies equally well in personal relationships. It's *"Givers gain."*

How to Be a Kinder, More Compassionate Person
No one is suggesting you turn yourself into the next Mother Theresa (although there is a vacancy). However, if you can't be bothered to make any effort to be special for someone else, you can't really expect anyone else to behave in a kind and compassionate way towards you. Teaching yourself to be a kinder person will make you a more appealing person. Especially if it hasn't been something you've ever thought much about before.

One of the most common obstacles to being kind and compassionate is insisting that you hold on tightly to all your past hurts and suffering. It is hard to be kind to others if you think they have been cruel to you. And yet, that is exactly what kindness is really about, and why the kindness feedback loop is so important.

Think briefly of all the people who have done you wrong, cheated or deceived you. Perhaps you even hate some of them. When you hate somebody else, it only hurts you. Many people find it very difficult to let go, our bruised egos refuse to 'let them get away with it'. So we hold on to those deep, painful emotions. We so often fail to realise that forgiveness is a liberating experience. To forgive someone doesn't mean you have to like them or make friends with them. Forgiveness helps you. It helps you to become less resentful. For some it purges their soul, releasing the potential to move forward in their lives, making the most of today and tomorrow. It clears away the dark clouds from their past. Many individuals who have suffered enormous prolonged abuse have successfully transformed their lives by letting go and forgiving those who hurt them.

Who could you forgive for whatever they did to you in the past? Do it today and notice how a great weight gets lifted from your shoulders. Forgive them whilst expecting nothing in return. They may not understand, they may not be grateful, they might not even care, but that's OK. You're doing it to be kind to yourself.

Most people are doing the best they can. So learn to be more patient and tolerant. Just because someone may fall short of your standards, it doesn't make them a bad person. Spot people doing good things and let them know you noticed. Help more people in your life to feel special about themselves. Learn how to let out your gorgeousness so others appreciate you more. The simplest and most effective way to do that is to help others let out their gorgeousness first.

Try developing another new habit of doing at least one kind deed every day without the recipient of your kindness or anybody else knowing. Notice how it makes you feel so much better about yourself. It is the most delicious feeling in the world to know that you've made somebody else's life on that day just a little bit better, without needing to be recognised or thanked for it. In a journal you might like to write down what you did and how these kindnesses made you feel about yourself. Rereading these notes in the future may help you remember what a good person you are.

Make a decision to give at least three genuine and sincere compliments to family, friends, colleagues and even some strangers. If someone is special, don't keep it to yourself. Make sure they know, too. Everybody needs reminding. So make a point of telling them how much you appreciate their friendship or something they may have done. If they deflect it away, look them straight in the eye and say: *"Please don't do that, it means a lot to me that you know how much I appreciate you."* Hug your friends more. And learn to relax when you do it. A hug should make you feel as though you're almost melting into each other. A hug is a sign of affection. It's not sexual.

Devote yourself to becoming a gold medal Olympic listener. Really listen. If you have to, bite your tongue until the other person finishes. That's not to say that you become everybody's 'audience'. Listening makes people feel special. Give people your undivided attention. Make them realise what they're saying is important to you. Encourage others (especially the quiet types) to open up. Be interested. The more you listen, the more others will love you for it.

As John Gray wrote in *Men are From Mars, Women are from Venus,* if a woman wants to talk about what's bothering her it doesn't necessarily mean she wants anyone to give her any advice (as well-meaning as they believe it might be). She probably just wants to be listened to. Give her your attention; help her feel 'heard'. Only offer solutions if you have been specifically asked to do so. And always accept that your advice and suggestions, however sensible they may be to you, do not have to be taken. The other person is always responsible for their own decisions. Forcing your opinions on other people is not kind.

For women: it's actually the same for men. They don't want to be told what to do either! Men also want to be heard, validated and respected.

Look for the good in others and you'll find it in yourself.

Notice the 'invisible' people. I once read an article about a homeless man who talked about the worst aspects of his situation. He didn't want to beg, so he spent hours trying to sell copies of *The Big Issue*, now sold by homeless people all over the world. In the article, the homeless man remarked that over 90% of the people who passed by would look through him as if he wasn't even there. I'm not saying you must always buy a copy, but see the person. Acknowledge the existence of everyone. A smile costs nothing. In Africa, there's a traditional greeting *"I see you." This means far more than "Hello." It's about recognising and respecting that person at a much deeper level.*

Imagine what it must be like to be the other people in your life. Appreciate the difficulties they experience. Empathise and understand. Always practise good manners. Simply say *"Please"* and *"Thank you"* more often. This is such basic stuff that gets ignored by so many. Yet politeness is free.

Penny Power, founder of Ecademy.com ensures she does

"A favour a day." Be dependable and reliable to everyone you know. Remind yourself of how many times and how many ways you have committed acts of kindness. And then keep it to yourself. Do good to be good.

The Penalties and Risks of Being 'Too' Kind

Can you be 'too' kind? Yes. Being a 'people pleaser' who is too accommodating and considerate in a relationship can have a negative longer-term effect on a partner who may learn to take advantage of such generosity. You may be seen as 'weak' if your partner thinks you are prepared to say *"Yes"* to every request. In some cases, the recipient learns to expect their own way all the time. Learn to say *"No"* when it's appropriate. Being kind is not the same as always agreeing to others' wishes.

Particularly kind men and women are often targeted by selfish 'users' and 'takers'. Who better to satisfy their ongoing hunger for getting what they want, than a 'giver'? When you are kind and compassionate, you tend to feel more for vulnerable people. And that includes those who have perfected the illusion of appearing vulnerable! Don't allow yourself to become a magnet for these men and women.

Unscrupulous 'takers' are fantastic at making you feel sorry for them (often when they absolutely don't deserve it). And they'll milk someone's generosity for as long as they can get away with it. Once found out, they simply move on to their next unsuspecting victim. They also rely on the 'giver's' high degree of trust to give them the benefit of any doubts. Indeed it's common for particularly kind people to feel guilty for even entertaining ideas that they are even being taken for a ride! Because a kind person thinks the best of others, he or she is unlikely to suspect they are being 'played'. Be alert.

Recognise and accept that you will be more appealing to some of the wrong people, but also to the right people. So be aware of the risks but don't let it stop you from improving the quality of life for those you know and care about. And listen more to your gut instinct. If you sense that someone is trying to take advantage of you, don't let them.

So, you might be thinking, if this is going to happen, doesn't it make sense to avoid being kind and compassionate in the first place? This way you protect yourself. No. The benefits of being a kind and compassionate person far outweigh any possible disadvantages.

Remember that just about everybody would choose to be with someone who has these kindness qualities. Kind people have become something of a rarity in this dog-eat-dog world. Be that person. But gently insist that any other person in your life needs to be, too.

A 'Wow' Solution

Years ago, I had moderated a particular conference. In the evening the client held a black tie dinner. Everybody dressed up in their smartest clothes. Men in tuxedos, the women in stunning ball gowns. One particular woman caught my eye. She wasn't going to win a beauty contest and was standing alone, near the middle of a fairly crowded bar area before we all went into dinner. It was obvious to me that she had really made an effort to look nice. It was a big night for her. She looked great. No one else seemed to have noticed her, though. So I walked towards her and as I passed by without stopping, I leaned over and whispered in her ear one word - *"Wow!"*

When I reached the other side of the room, I looked back to see this woman glowing! It was incredible. This is the power of being noticed and appreciated without having a personal agenda.

Just for fun I then came up with the idea of creating a small card with "Wow" in large letters on one side. On the other side was a brief note explaining why it had been given. There's more information about these cards at the back of this book. It's so interesting to observe how people respond to this fun idea. The majority 'get it' instantly. Their faces light up. They think the cards are a great idea. Becky, one of my colleagues, just loves to watch a guy's face when she unexpectedly hands out one of these cards. If everyone gave them out to just about anybody, their specialness would be diminished. Because they are rare, their 'currency' value remains quite high.

Yet a small minority of men and women respond negatively. They regard them as cheesy, insincere, or even as one person put it, a form of 'stalking'. They seem so completely closed to any attempt at showing appreciation to others.

Some recipients have told me they laminated the card they had been given and stuck it up on their dressing table mirror as a daily reminder to themselves that they have been noticed and appreciated. Check out WowCardz.com if you'd like to pick up a pack of these cards.

One night at an Irish restaurant my female companion and I couldn't help being particularly impressed at the service from our waitress. She was in her fifties, with a fantastic personality. A real character who made interesting conversation and knowledgeably advised us what was good on the menu (and, in fact, at one point what **not** to order). She was the perfect hostess. My friend suggested she qualified for a Wow card. I had one on me and the next time she came to our table, I presented it on behalf of us both. She was puzzled at first. So I suggested she take it away and read the back of the card when she had a moment.

Only a few minutes later she came back. She was quite overwhelmed. And kept saying: *"Thank you so much. You have no idea how much this means to me. Thank you. Thank you."* Here was someone who obviously appreciated the card, and the thinking behind it.

At the end of the meal, she brought us the bill. We paid and stood up to leave. The waitress kissed me on the cheek and hugged my friend. When we got back to the car I said: *"What did she whisper to you when she gave you that hug?"* She paused a moment and said quietly: *"This morning she received confirmation that she has cancer."*

You just never know how much of an effect even a small act of kindness can have.

Daily Stop and Start Reminders

Stop

- ☐ Stop criticising yourself. It wouldn't be kind if you did it to another person, and it isn't kind to you.
- ☐ Stop giving yourself such a hard time for not living up to this vision of perfection you have created for yourself.
- ☐ Kind and compassionate people don't punish, even when the guilty may actually deserve it. Cruelty of any type is never cool.
- ☐ Therefore, never mistreat any animal. Truly kind people do not mistreat anyone or anything.
- ☐ Banish all harsh and critical words from your vocabulary.
- ☐ Eliminate 'hate'. Hating somebody else only ever harms you. Any hate you hold in your heart crowds out love.
- ☐ Stop thinking you can change anybody else. Start with yourself instead.
- ☐ Don't judge or criticise. It might make you feel better about yourself, but at the expense of those you judge and criticise. They will like you less, even if you believe passionately that you are right and they are wrong.
- ☐ Stop taking people for granted. Appreciate others more.
- ☐ A big part of being kind to yourself is the ability to move on. Do not cling on to what 'could have been'. What was, was. What is, is.
- ☐ Stop taking everything so personally and holding on to it. My dear friend Paul McGee is author of *SUMO* – which stands for *"Shut Up and Move On!"*

Start

- ☐ Look after yourself better. Enough sleep, good food, plenty of water.
- ☐ Be kind to yourself in as many ways as you can come up with – but never at the expense of anyone else.
- ☐ Be quick to praise and slow to criticise.
- ☐ Help other people look good, without ever letting yourself look bad.
- ☐ Listen carefully to what people enjoy. Use that information to help you select the perfect gift the next time their birthday or Christmas comes around.
- ☐ Offer genuine encouragement to others.
- ☐ Say more nice things.
- ☐ Say *"Thank you"* at least 10 times a day. And mean it. Look the person in the eye when you say it. Make sure they know you're being sincere.
- ☐ If somebody tells you something good about a friend or a colleague, tell that friend or colleague what you heard. If you heard something bad, don't pass it on.
- ☐ Become known for your discretion. If you're told a secret, make absolutely sure it stays a secret.
- ☐ Whenever you think fondly of a friend, call or e-mail to tell them. Better still, send them a handwritten note. You may discover they keep and cherish such notes for years.
- ☐ Be more aware of your tone of voice when discussing sensitive issues. What you say and what others hear are often very different.
- ☐ Laugh with people, never at them.
- ☐ If you're a loud person most of the time, learn to lower the volume. And step back from the limelight occasionally. It shows respect. Others will feel more valued and appreciated.
- ☐ Decide to make people feel at ease with themselves.

- ☐ Practise empathy by asking yourself what it would be like to be the person you are with.
- ☐ Work hard to increase the proportion of time you are aware of the needs of others.
- ☐ Remind yourself of how many times and how many ways you have committed acts of kindness. But keep it to yourself. Its effect gets diluted when you tell others how wonderful you've been!
- ☐ Practise random acts of kindness. If the recipient of your kind act really appreciated it and tries to repay you, ask them to do small favours for complete strangers instead. This way your initial kindness gets multiplied by getting 'paid forward'.
- ☐ Get involved in voluntary or charitable work. It makes you feel better about yourself whilst helping others less fortunate.
- ☐ Make the conscious decision to deepen your friendships by creating a safe environment for people to be open with you.

"Nobody cares how much you know, until they know how much you care." Cavett Robert (Founder, National Speakers Association)

Chapter 10

Intimacy

Developing your Emotional Core is key to becoming the 'you' with the inner-strength and self-assurance to be The One for someone else. A successful relationship is down to the way individuals choose to come together to create a unit, made up of two distinct pieces: you and them, plus a third, which is you 'the couple'. This unit is largely based on intimacy. In this chapter we focus on how to develop true intimacy, which in turn creates the best environment for long-term mutual happiness.

Part of the Emotional Core strengthening process is about gaining a deeper, more intimate, yet clearer understanding of yourself: any helpful and unhelpful patterns of thinking, how those thoughts affect your behaviour and how all of that is linked to the relationship results you have enjoyed or endured in the past.

If you have taken the time to answer the questions, thought about the ideas presented in this book so far and worked on the Emotional Core components most relevant to you, you may have noticed slight, or even major shifts in the way you think and feel about yourself. Perhaps you are far more at peace with yourself. And now have a happier and more intimate relationship with yourself. I hope so.

Developing your Emotional Core is all about you. True intimacy, commitment and love are about your relationship with someone else.

As you strengthen your Emotional Core, you build up your capacity to be emotionally intimate. Intimacy exists on so many levels: physically and emotionally. Sexual intimacy tends to be the first level that usually comes to mind. However, intimacy is far more than just sex. A great deal of our comfort level with a partner is linked to physical, non-sexual contact.

Recently I was chatting with my brother Mike, and Julie, his wife. They had just celebrated their Silver wedding anniversary. As we talked, I noticed how Mike was running his hand up and down her back. It wasn't just touching to see, it showed the strong bond that still exists between them after 25 years of marriage. I'm not even sure whether either of them were even consciously aware that it was happening. Yet so many adults stop touching, sometimes afraid that it will be misinterpreted and unwelcome.

Physical touch is a fundamental human need. Allowing or encouraging someone to touch you is an act of intimacy. Occasional, non-sexual touching is an important ingredient for any long-term loving relationship. Brushing past your partner, stroking them in reassuring ways all combine to re-affirm the intimate bond that has been established between you.

Sex, Lust and Passion

For some reason, at this point I feel compelled to share these two jokes:

> Q. What's an Australian kiss?
> A. It's exactly the same as a French Kiss. But it's 'down-under'.

> It's thought that the first words ever uttered in the Garden of Eden were sex-related. Apparently Adam said to Eve: *"Stand back. I don't know how big this thing gets."* Eve then waited and waited. And in so doing, became the world's first disappointed woman.

Sex can be funny. Especially if you're doing it with the right person.

For many, the potential for one-night stands and casual sexual flings dominate their lives. He wants to be successful with a woman. She wants someone to want and desire her. In a very real sense, casual sex partners exchange their short-term sexual needs: two lonely people using each other's bodies to provide localised friction. Yes, the physical sensations and release of tension can feel great at the time. The thrill, excitement and passion. Sometimes made even more potent for being 'forbidden fruit'. Yet in so many cases those feelings are quickly followed by a sense of emptiness. Certainly not feelings of having shared something deeply intimate with someone important. For the sexually active person who is not in a committed monogamous relationship, having sexual intercourse is often only about finding someone who will say 'yes'.

It becomes sport. It's about scoring. It's certainly not true intimacy. It's more like a counterfeit Rolex watch; a cheap version of something with world-class quality. The more casual sex partners someone has had, the more likely it is that they will think of sex as merely a physical activity. The intimate emotional connection disappears, if it was ever there. For some, sex even gets in the way of intimacy. They fail to realise that true intimacy is far more than sexual intercourse.

For a variety of religious and societal reasons millions of people have been conditioned to think of sex as shameful, degrading and sinful. Understanding your own attitudes towards intimacy and sex can be very illuminating. So ask yourself these questions:

- How much is sex only about satisfying your own carnal needs?
- After sex, how much better do you feel about yourself?
- Or do you experience feeling 'dirty' about what you just did?
- Do you have a history of slinking away into the night afterwards? Or doing the aptly named 'walk of shame' the following morning?
- How much do you care about what it was like for your sexual partner?
- Is sex something that tends to get 'done' to you? Or is it something you just want to 'do' to someone else?
- What proportion of the time you are having sex do you focus on discovering and/or satisfying the needs of your partner?

Until both partners in a sexual relationship commit themselves to ***giving*** pleasure, true intimacy will remain elusive.

Wanting to go to bed with someone can be intoxicatingly potent. However, how much you want to wake up with that person can be far more insightful.

This is not a sex manual. Learning more about the sexual needs of each other will increase the levels of intimacy in almost every loving relationship. For all sorts of reasons it can be difficult to persuade a partner to say what they like or don't like. Therefore:

- Learn how to give non-sexual massages to each other. As expertise improves and confidence grows, with mutual permission explore more intimate forms of massage.
- Play the More/Less Game. Take it in turns to touch, stroke, fondle, kiss, lick and stimulate each other. Whatever is being done, you or your partner says whether you want them to

do it 'more' or 'less'. In this way you can get to know each other's likes and dislikes very easily. And in a safe, secure and trusting environment. Don't do what they don't like. Do what they do. Play this game and I challenge you not to laugh together at some point. This in itself improves intimacy further.

Barriers to Intimacy

In much the same way we studied unhappiness to better understand happiness, knowing how we mess up intimacy can be rather helpful too. Without intimacy, a long-term, happy relationship cannot be sustained.

Money worries are a major contributing factor to a couple's ability and desire to be intimate. According to research held by the Consumer Financial Education Body (CFEB) , individuals who exercise financial responsibility experience an increase in their psychological well-being and life satisfaction. This in turn decreases the potential for feelings of anxiety and depression. In a YouGov survey commissioned by Relate, men are twice as likely as women to be concerned that money worries will cause them to break up with their partner. One in five couples felt they were arguing more because of money worries. To maintain intimacy within a harmonious relationship, financial compatibility is crucial. Sharing financial responsibilities and mutually respecting each other's feelings about money is similarly essential.

> *"My wife and I keep fighting about sex and money. I think she charges me too much."* Rodney Dangerfield (Comedian)

A relationship is like a valuable vase: it has the capacity to hold anything you choose to put into it. The vase can be as large as you and your partner want it to be. But you both need to look after it. It's inevitable that on occasions it will get damaged. And with children around, the vase needs even more protection.

In today's throwaway society we are sometimes too quick to replace the old, but still perfectly functional, with a newer model. Over time all of our relationships get damaged at least occasionally. Sometimes that damage is extensive and seemingly irreparable. In those situations, you and your partner will be forced to decide what to do about your time-worn, damaged vase. You have various options: carry on living without putting anything new in the vase or leave it broken and carry on using it as if nothing had happened. But if you both take your relationship seriously you'll choose another option: to apply effort and skill into repairing and maintaining it.

The glue you use to repair a relationship vase is like those where you mix two compounds. Bringing them into direct contact with one another is the catalyst for starting a chemical reaction, which leads to an incredibly strong bond. The active ingredients for relationship repair are true intimacy and commitment. Physical intimacy is what usually starts it all; commitment is for longer-term strength and effectiveness. One without the other can lead ultimately to the old cracks reappearing.

What about relationships that are working well? Even then it's easy to fall into the trap of 'coasting'. Not bothering. Taking everything and each other for granted. When the sun is shining, it's tempting to sit out in a garden with a cool drink, listening to your music player, blissfully unaware that slowly and imperceptibly the weeds are growing around you. Any gardener will tell you that regular weeding is essential if you're going to ensure they don't take over. Weeds in the form of arguments and disagreements do this if left unattended. In a relationship, they choke intimacy.

Disagreements are a natural part of any healthy relationship. In fact, it worries me a little whenever I hear new couples proudly tell me *"We never argue. Ever."* I suspect that in some of those cases, important differences don't get aired, sometimes for a 'quieter life'. At the other extreme, some relationships are fiery and constantly argumentative. There's competition within the relationship. I know of one such relationship where they were at each others' throats most of the time. They made a point of telling everyone that it worked because the 'make up sex' was so good. Eventually they wore each other out and split up. Apparently, it was the arguing that ground them down, not the sex.

Teenagers tend to choose boyfriends and girlfriends who are most like them. It's a bit like *"I love me. Therefore I will 'love' someone who is the most like me."* But as we grow older, we start to realise that partners who are different yet share the same core values, beliefs and life aspirations have the capacity to bring richness, interest and diversity into our lives. With that diversity, however, also comes the increased potential for conflict and disagreement. Constant arguing, bickering and conflict obviously don't lend themselves to long-term harmony, happiness and intimacy. How you both repair these rifts is at the heart of it.

What distinguishes a relationship that works from one that doesn't? It isn't that they have no arguments; it is how those differences get resolved. Knowing how to repair disagreements is a major life skill. And it's something that both partners need to take equal responsibility for. If you are the only person who does the repairing all the time, ultimately the relationship will suffer because it becomes so one-sided.

Personality Types

The world would be a boring place if everybody was the same. We're not. Understanding that is key to resolving your differences rather than letting them fester.

In 1921, Swiss psychiatrist Carl Jung published *Psychological Types*, the first fully developed categorisation of personality types. Psychologists Shay and Margaret McConnon have graciously given me permission to summarise their own extensive work on personality types and conflict resolution. They have simplified Jung's personality types as:

1) The Go-Getter
2) The Carer
3) The Analyser
4) The Socialiser

We all have some of each, but tend to have a preferred or dominant personality type. None are better or worse than any of the others. They are just different.

The Go-Getter is on a mission to succeed, to win and get things done quickly. They are direct, decisive, to-the-point, very results-driven, work well to deadlines and don't suffer fools gladly. They work hard and play hard. And are likely to be attracted to extreme sports for the 'buzz' they get from adrenaline.

The Carer is warm, friendly, very good at building rapport and trust. They make time for others, are excellent listeners, are thoughtful, loyal and co-operative. They don't like conflict and tend not to criticise or judge others. Relationships are particularly important to Carers.

The Analyser is often a perfectionist, paying meticulous attention to detail. Things have to be 'right'. They like to be in control and tend not to delegate for fear of others getting things 'wrong'. Careful and risk-averse, routinely they notice what's wrong and foresee problems. They are logical and will base decisions on proof or evidence, and rarely if ever on 'gut instinct'. They are independent, don't need others and therefore are not usually team players.

The Socialiser is relaxed, easy-going, positive, enthusiastic, energetic and open to new ideas. They can be highly creative, confident to go with their 'gut' regardless of the consequences, are visionary, innovative and they like variety. They have a well-developed sense of humour, enjoy having fun and mix well.

When relationships are running smoothly most of the above qualities are perceived as positives. However, when a personal, professional or intimate relationship hits problems, a person's previously perceived positives seem to morph into negatives.

The Go-Getter is then seen by the aggrieved party as arrogant, pushy, overpowering, a bully, intolerant and impatient. Too busy to sit down and talk things through, they've already got the answers so what's the point talking about anything. They decide that such discussions are a waste of time.
The Carer may be seen as taking things 'far too personally', is submissive, weak, too 'soft' and way too gullible. They have an annoying tendency to want to hug and hold someone when that's the *last* thing the other person wants.
The Analyser can be perceived as cold, unfriendly, dysfunctionally independent, controlling, intolerant, inflexible, judgemental, intensely negative, pedantic. It's probably not a coincidence that the first four letters of this personality type spells 'anal'.
The Socialiser now seems disorganised, illogical, never thinks things through, thinks out loud, seeks consensus so takes forever to reach a decision, starts too much and finishes too little. They are flippant, everything is a 'joke' to them, and they are irritatingly positive all the damn time!!!

Which type or types are you? Who have you worked with who fits each of these different personality types? And how have you tended to get on with them in the past? Now think about current and past intimate relationships. How did the above personality type differences influence how your relationship worked or didn't work?

In many cases people are not even aware of their own personality type, never mind anyone else's. Just realising that others might have a different personality can help us to accept them for who they are. This can have a profound and positive impact on our own ability to get on better with them. You can therefore become far more compatible with a broader range of people. Without possessing this basic understanding of personality types, coping with personality differences can be very stressful. You can imagine the damage this does to the potential for intimacy.

How you manage the natural disagreements, misunderstandings and conflicts of a relationship defines its chances of long-term success. That is why it is so valuable to be fully aware, ahead of time, of how to recognise differences of opinions at an earlier stage, and have strategies to minimise their effects.

'First' or 'Second' Position

Most people see life through what psychologists call 'first position': through our own eyes, our own position. Most of us tend to assume that everyone else sees things in exactly the same way we see them. We assume our priorities 'should' be someone else's priorities. Because the 'first position' is our own, we tend to assume it is 'right'. Anything else that differs from this 'first position' is therefore probably 'wrong' - in our own minds, at least.

At one end of a 'stubbornness scale', bigots, racists and 'difficult' people absolutely cannot and will not accept that any view other than their own has any merit whatsoever. They have an extreme level of inflexibility, intolerance and arrogance. They won't accept that someone else's view or behaviour is just as valid as their own.

'Second position' is the mental capacity to see, feel and perceive life from another person's perspective. 'Second position' leads to understanding and accepting that the other person has a view that may be different to our own, and acknowledging that this does not make them 'wrong'. It's just different. On the other end of the scale mentioned above, some people cannot move out of 'second position'. They have locked themselves into the belief that everyone else is more important than they are; the views of others are more valid than their own. Emotionally healthy people will be near the middle of the scale and are comfortable moving back and forth between 'first' and 'second' position.

'First position' is also how people tend to express their love or appreciation for a partner. In other words, they demonstrate their love in the way they would most want love to be expressed to them. For example, if they want to hear their partner tell them how much they are loved, in order to feel deeply loved or appreciated, that's what they will do to their partner. Even if their partner might prefer to be hugged. In the million selling book *The Five Love Languages* Gary Chapman PhD describes how to keep 'the love tank full' by knowing and switching to your partner's preferred love language:

1) Words of affirmation
2) Quality time
3) Receiving gifts
4) Acts of service
5) Physical touch.

When you want a partner to feel deeply loved and appreciated, don't express it the way you would want to hear it. Express it the way they want to experience it. You may feel loved when your partner gives you a gift, but don't be disappointed if the gift you give them is met with semi-indifference. It does not mean they didn't care about your gift of love, it just means that they didn't necessarily understand the significance you had attached to it. It's almost as if you had said something to them in another language. But when you learn to 'speak' their love language, the reaction will be very different. Another example: if words are important to your partner, telling them or writing about how proud you are of something they did can mean the world to them.

When you feel love, you feel it in 'first position', but expressing love to your partner has to be done in 'second position'. A long-term, mutually happy relationship requires both parties to have the desire and ability to switch between 'first' and 'second' position whenever it's appropriate.

ABCs – Arguing, Blaming and Conflict

Almost all arguing, blaming and conflict is as a result of 'first position' thinking. If either or both parties have underdeveloped Emotional Cores too, their reactions to those with different personality types will often trigger feelings of intimidation and defensiveness. Feeling they are being 'attacked', abused, patronised and disrespected, even when they are not, is quite common. Miscommunication and further misunderstanding becomes even more likely as each party either withdraws into a position of defence, or goes on the attack. All this has the potential for lots of misunderstanding.

Someone with an underdeveloped Emotional Core is far more likely to have an emotional farting fit (as described in Chapter 4) during a row or a disagreement. This further increases the likelihood that the argument will escalate out of control. Not talking about the little things over time leads to much bigger unresolved issues. If it happens often enough, the relationship may breakdown permanently. Intimacy can't happen in such an environment.

Understanding how to resolve conflict and disagreement without 'caving in' to the other person every time has enormous power to remove one of the largest barriers to intimacy.

Keep in mind that it is impossible to win an argument with your intimate partner. Even if you seem to 'win', you both always 'lose'. Using your verbal dexterity to beat your opponent just means you will pay later. In some way. Because if they are your opponent, they cannot be your partner. Resentment and hurt builds inside you or your partner, only to surface in different ways sometime in the future. Demonstrating how and why a partner is 'wrong' and why you or they are 'right' also kills intimacy. Winning may make you feel stronger, however, the relationship will always be weakened as a consequence in the longer term.

How you each argue, what you feel you need to prove to yourself and the other person, all stem from the relationship you have with yourself and the state of your Emotional Core. Anyone with low self-esteem or underlying unhappiness will eventually get provoked into lashing out. And it won't have anything to do with who didn't put the top on the toothpaste!

In *The Seven Principles for Making Marriage Work*, authors John Gottman and Nan Silver describe how a happy couple's 'repair attempts' are a secret weapon. Their detailed research confirms that this is one of the primary factors in determining whether a relationship thrives or dies. It's the couple's shared friendship, mutual respect and their joint commitment to the relationship that motivates them to adopt strategies that help them to repair rather than merely 'patch-up' their disagreements.

They become experts when it comes to mending their relationship vase. Happy couples repair strategies that strengthen, rather than weaken their relationships. This is not the case with unhappy, self-centred individuals with low self-esteem, a poor attitude and an unkind disposition; they are prepared to fight dirty in times of conflict. They don't care about the longer-term consequences of their behaviour because crushing their opponent is all that matters in that moment.

In so many cases such men and women are also the first to complain (often very loudly) that everybody else is being difficult because they won't do what they are being told. They tend to be the only person who isn't aware that they're the one who is being arrogant and unreasonable. Are there times when you can be like that? Is it possible that it is you who is sometimes at least part of the root cause of the problems you complain so loudly about? Just because someone else won't do what you tell them, doesn't mean that they are automatically wrong. Proving you are right and they are wrong, however, won't help you longer term.

If you have differences, keeping quiet about them isn't a solution either. Like a pressure cooker that's left unsupervised on a high heat, one day it will explode. Therefore it is essential for both parties to let off steam occasionally. Precisely how this is done is critically important.

Well before either of you 'blows-up', if you are irritated by something about your partner, first try to figure out if the cause of your irritation is actually something else. And don't ask your friends. Based on what you choose to tell them (or not tell them), they'll probably agree with you because they want you to feel better. It's possible that the real cause of the problem has nothing to do with your partner. Therefore taking it out on someone innocent isn't ever going to help you. Or your relationship.

If there are differences that need to be sorted out with a partner, here, with their permission, are some thoughts and effective strategies, courtesy of psychologists Shay and Margaret McConnon from their book *Resolving Conflict*:

- There is nothing inherently wrong with either of you for having differences. However, there could be something wrong about 'us'. To resolve conflict you have to think as an 'us'. 'You' and 'me' need to become a 'we'.
- Accept that you are creating conflict if you insist that others conform to your values and needs, at their expense. Conflict is created by others if your values and needs are being ignored.
- If something is important to you, it doesn't mean that it is necessarily important to anyone else.
- Anyone who uses words like you 'should', 'must', 'have to' is saying that they are more important than the other person.
- Nothing will be gained by attacking, and there's everything to lose. Fight the problem, not the person.
- Once you attack you have lost all chance of having a willing collaboration.

- Listen. Really listen. Let the other person speak without interruption. Don't tell them how wrong they are. Shut up until they've run out of steam or they finish.
- You can show you are not listening by finishing somebody else's sentences. Don't do it. Even though you might be convinced that you know what they're going to say. All too often we are wrong.
- Put aside what anyone is saying or doing and ask yourself and the other person what is the 'positive intention'? It is possible that either you or the other person is simply misinterpreting or misunderstanding that intention, which may in reality, be quite innocent or well-meaning.
- Gaining a better understanding of someone's motives for their actions, without judging or criticising them, is always the best place to start. Asking a low-key, non-confrontational question can be a good opener such as: *"I may be misunderstanding what's going on here. Please can you explain it to me?"*
- You have a choice: focus all your energy on the 'problems' or you can each concentrate on finding solutions that work for both of you.
- Win-lose is always a weak solution. Win-win is always stronger. This can only occur if the needs of both are satisfied. Most people fear losing something. Remove that fear. Focus on their needs as a way of satisfying yours.
- Part of this is being partners not opponents.
- At the end, if either party feels 'beaten', you both lose.
- If you both agree on a course of action, stick to it. Keep your word.

Resolving conflicts and disagreements together can strengthen a relationship, increase levels of mutual understanding, appreciation, respect and trust. Over time, if these qualities are nurtured and allowed to grow equally between two mature people, a deep mutual commitment is formed.

The Most Effective Intimacy Enhancer

> *"One of the best ways to persuade others is with your ears – by listening to them."* Dean Rusk (Former US Secretary of State)

The most effective way to build intimacy with a partner is to give them your full, undivided attention. Stop reading. Turn off the TV. Look at your partner and allow them to open up to you in a safe environment. They need to know you will really listen, without judging, criticising or telling them what they should do. Only offer solutions if you have been told specifically that this is what they want. And they must know that whatever is said, is not only confidential but will never get used as 'ammunition' in a future argument. Just listen. Be understanding. Make them know how much you care and that they are worth your full attention.

Everyone needs or appreciates at least some TLC. That's the topic for the next chapter. In this case TLC stands for Trust, Love and Commitment.

Stop and Start Reminders

Stop

- ☐ Stop dragging bad experiences around with you to every new relationship.
- ☐ Never talk about ex-partners. Don't even say anything bad about them. Your current partner will fear that this is how you'd talk about them if things don't work out between you. And *never* tell a partner anything about your sex life with a former partner. No exceptions.
- ☐ Similarly, never make derogatory remarks about your partner's sexual ability. The implication is that you are making comparisons with former lovers. It will stick in their memory forever.
- ☐ Stop criticising the opposite sex generally. All women and all men are not the same. Avoid anyone who constantly whinges and complains about the opposite sex.
- ☐ When you're wrong, learn to shut up and listen. If appropriate say *"I'm sorry."* And mean it.
- ☐ Don't let things stew. If you have a problem, say so. Be assertive and find solutions earlier rather than later.
- ☐ Don't assume you are telepathic and 'know 'what your partner is thinking. If confused, quietly and in a non-threatening and non-accusing way, ask the person to tell you what they mean.
- ☐ Don't assume your partner is telepathic and knows what you are thinking. The rule is simple: *"If you don't say it, they don't know it."*
- ☐ Stop blaming anyone else for the way you feel. Your emotions are your responsibility, no one else's.
- ☐ Stop insisting that every facet of even the tiniest problems needs to be discussed.
- ☐ Stop keeping score. Because in a relationship no

matter how many points you or your partner have scored, you both lose! Point scoring is always bad for a relationship.

- ☐ Stop shouting. It is verbal anger. Anger is corrosive. Sarcasm is even worse. Cut it out of your life.
- ☐ Never roll your eyes at your partner, friends or your colleagues. Tapping your fingers is also extremely disrespectful.
- ☐ Never belittle anyone in public. Stop making your partner (or anyone else for that matter) the butt of your jokes.
- ☐ Stop swearing. It is never cool. No one is ever impressed by it, and it just cheapens you.
- ☐ Don't be cruel in the interest of *"Telling the truth."*
- ☐ Don't dress up criticism to appear as if it is well-meaning advice. Especially advice that has not been asked for.
- ☐ Never nag.
- ☐ Television is a conversation killer. Switch it off occasionally. Some people enjoy media-free days. No television, no radio, no newspapers and no magazines. Just each other. Try it.
- ☐ Don't test your relationship to find out how much they care about you.
- ☐ Wanting to be with someone to the exclusion of all others is not healthy behaviour. And it can be intensely suffocating for the other party.
- ☐ It's unrealistic to expect even the most perfect person in the world to share all of your interests. Develop a team of friends who you can enjoy the activities your partner isn't as enthusiastic about as you. Get a life outside your relationship and encourage your partner to do so, too.
- ☐ Stop trying to fix somebody who isn't right for you. Water doesn't argue with the slope, it flows with it. Pushing water uphill is the way we often try to control our relationships. It's pointless.

- ☐ Realise that just because you don't like something a partner does, it does not by definition mean they are trying to hurt or upset you.
- ☐ You have a right to know what the other person thinks of you. You don't have the right to make demands.
- ☐ Making someone else feel bad because you are is never justified.
- ☐ Don't make conditions or issue threats. Ever.
- ☐ Stop giving others the silent treatment.
- ☐ Do not become an unpaid carer for someone who's got real problems of a psychological or chemical basis. If your response is: "*But I love them and want to look after them.*" Buy a dog.

Start

- ☐ You can change or improve anything about yourself or your situation if you want to do so strongly enough. That doesn't include other people.
- ☐ Ask people who have really good relationships why they believe it works. Listen and learn.
- ☐ It's difficult to feel happy when you are over-tired or exhausted. Get enough sleep.
- ☐ Go to bed with your partner at the same time.
- ☐ Say *"please"* and *"thank you"* to your partner more often.
- ☐ Give your time, attention and energy to those who deserve it.
- ☐ Some people don't deserve respect. Give it to them anyway.
- ☐ Be more proactive. How much time are you squandering standing in the waiting room of your own life?
- ☐ Offer your unconditional support to friends, family and colleagues.
- ☐ Become someone who is known for their encouraging words.
- ☐ Clear the air with kindness.
- ☐ Be lovable. Always.
- ☐ We have two ears and one mouth. Use them in that proportion.
- ☐ If you're a naturally gregarious person, try something new; instead of doing all the talking, consciously decide to do more listening.
- ☐ People need to know at the deepest possible level that they are appreciated, respected, loved and adored. Some are not used to this so it can take a long time. You can't just tell them once: everybody needs reminding.
- ☐ Encourage each other to enjoy life as a child does.

- ☐ Energy flows in and out of our bodies, all the time. Become more aware of what energises you and what de-energises you. Focus more on the former, and less on the latter.
- ☐ Encourage your partner to talk more about themselves. And listen. When it's your turn, take up less time than they did.
- ☐ Learn to be more concise.
- ☐ Focus on the problem not the person.
- ☐ Savour the moment and fully appreciate where you are, who you're with and how lucky you are.
- ☐ Take the initiative to build a future together.
- ☐ Set out to share new experiences.
- ☐ Create a bank of shared memories. This builds a stronger future bond and links the relationship to good stuff rather than what is dull or mundane.
- ☐ Walk alongside each other, rather than in front or behind.
- ☐ Remind yourself regularly why you fell in love with your partner.

Chapter 11

TLC - Trust, Love & Commitment

In some versions of ancient Taoist philosophy, it is taught that there are 36,000 gods and goddesses in the body. They leave us in disgust if we eat badly, drink excessively, disrespect ourselves and allow our minds to become cesspools of thought. Taoists also describe life as a journey. It's the 'big picture' shared by us all. A spiritual dimension provides an even bigger picture.

Through sunshine and storms, with distractions, delays and disappointments along the way, we all walk towards old age. Sometimes we walk as part of a group, sometimes alone or sometimes with a companion. Occasionally we travel with someone we would be better off without, and for longer than is good for us, but we tolerate them perhaps for fear of the alternative: being alone. And at other times, companions decide to head off in another direction or travel with someone else. It happens all the time and isn't good or bad, it just is.

We sometimes walk ahead, a few steps behind or if they're special, alongside each other hand-in-hand. If we're really lucky that special person is someone we will get to know over time by developing a deep, genuine friendship based on trust and mutual respect. With a shared sense of where you both want to go in life, with compatible goals and aspirations, you enjoy the richness of each other's company so much that you jointly decide to travel on your journey together forever.

In today's fast-paced world, our life journey may not be on foot any more. We're more likely to take the car. Some people focus on who they are with, while others are less interested in the companion and far more preoccupied with the make and model of the car, and what those cars will be in the future.

As far as our relationships are concerned, we can set the cruise control, put on the air conditioning and let everything take care of itself. Everything is fine so long as the road is straight and you don't hit anything, or let anything hit you. But more interesting journeys require effort and attention. And, as in the happiest and most rewarding relationships, both partners share the driving. No one is always the passenger. No one is always the driver.

Bumps, dents and scratches are inevitable. Smash-ups also happen even to the most careful drivers. Responsible behaviour will minimise the risks but they can never be eliminated altogether. Those who decide to travel together learn to trust each other implicitly. If or when that trust is broken, any relationship, especially intimate ones, can take years to recover. Some never do.

Trust

It's been said that if a woman isn't prepared to commit, she's 'independent'. If a man won't commit he's labelled 'commitment phobic'. Neither is true.

At the root of any relationship that lacks commitment there's a trust issue. Failing to trust our own judgement based on poor past partner choices is a very common reason to resist commitment. Such people just aren't sure what they think and feel about themselves or their partner is correct. After all, they've been wrong before: perhaps many times. In addition to this they might sense their partner is pushing them into making a commitment before they've made up their own mind.

Feeling that you are part of someone else's agenda will also stand in the way of commitment. As politically incorrect as it might appear, this has to be stated: more and more men in particular are becoming increasingly nervous about getting married when they see a conveyor belt of high-profile divorces in the media in which the men are financially skewered by the courts. Men cannot help fearing that they'll work hard, become the success they aspire to and then have it all taken away if they marry the wrong woman. They are worried. And genuine, sincere and kind women are suffering because of the behaviour of a few ball-breaking, deceitful women. As negative as this may sound, men and women need to be more careful than ever before about who they trust and who they commit to.

There are two sides to trust. Being trustworthy and being too trusting. Let's look at the latter first.

Too Trusting

People who are too trusting are sometimes targeted by unscrupulous men and women because they are easy victims. If you are a particularly trusting person, without trying to turn you into a cynic, be alert to the following ploys, especially at the beginning of a new relationship:

- Have you been told things about your partner's past that make you feel sorry for them? Unscrupulous people are brilliant at doing this.
- Are those incidents difficult to prove or challenge? Or would you feel callous asking them to do so? This is another common tactic they use.
- Do they have a habit of 'forgetting' their wallet or purse and asking you to lend them small amounts of cash? If so, they might be testing you to see how generous you are and how easy you are to manipulate.
- Do things regularly 'crop up' at the last minute as their excuse for not showing up or being massively late?

- Are they overly secretive about even the smallest, relatively insignificant things?
- Does your gut instinct tell you that something is not quite right about them, but because they are so appealing in other ways, you choose to ignore it?

Any one of these traits isn't enough to eliminate someone from your life, but clusters of these behaviours should be a cause for concern. Listen to your instinct.

Being Trustworthy

This is like a savings account. Over a long period you make small and larger deposits into this personal trust fund. Being trustworthy is never about what you say or promise, or about how 'nice' you are, it's what you do. This is achieved by being reliable and dependable, consistent, faithful and supportive. Being predictable is sometimes seen as a bit boring: in this context it certainly isn't.

Trustworthy people create a safe environment in which others open up, because they keep secrets and never misuse anything they are ever told in confidence. They are not gossips. They have nothing to hide about themselves. They are fair, discreet, tactful and treat people well. They will defend and protect their family, friends and their lover and never take advantage of people or situations. They tell the truth always. They don't lie by omission as honesty is important to them. When they make promises, they keep them. They are happy to share their own dreams, aspirations and vulnerabilities. And accept full responsibility for who they are and the decisions they make.

Above all they know that trust is earned, it isn't merely 'granted'. They have integrity, which has been defined as *"What you do when no one else is watching."* All these qualities become the backbone of a trustworthy person.

Untrustworthy individuals are none of these things. They often feel they 'can't help themselves' and claim to be slaves to their emotions and short-term cravings. They're incapable of delaying gratification and are prepared to sacrifice long-term happiness and stability for life's short cuts and shallow pleasures. Which as we all know, can be very difficult to resist. Yet trustworthy people can and do resist the same temptations.

Trust is a full-time job: it can't be part-time.

L- Love

What words would you use to describe your current understanding of what 'love' means? Write them below. Do it before you read any further.

Now, answer these questions yourself or with a friend:

- What's the difference between 'infatuation' and being 'in love'?
- What's the difference between 'falling in love' and 'being in love'?
- What happens at a scientific level when you are attracted to someone or when you fall in love?
- How many different types of love are there?
- Is love a 'feeling' or a series of 'actions'?

The rest of this section addresses elements of the above, but the point is that the more you think about the answers to these questions, the more confusing the subject can become. Love is a word that has become so over-used, we're not really that clear any more about what it is. Yet you'd think that living in a society dominated by so much talk of love and how widely it is spread through fairy tales, love songs, romantic comedies, newspaper and magazine articles, radio and TV shows that an accurate definition would be easy. But it isn't.

You can 'love' a dog, a special piece of jewellery, the latest gadget you've bought, your car, friends, parents, children, your god, your favourite food and your lover. These kinds of love all exist. But they are all different, too. Loving an object is obviously different to loving a person. And as we will see below, there are numerous forms of love we experience with the people we know and care about. Not all of them lead to long-term happiness though.

Romantic Love and Passion

Look back over the words you chose to define love. How many of them are based on aspects of 'romantic love'? If that's the case, you're not alone. Most people do the same. Romantic love gets nearly all the attention, so it's inevitable that most of us think of love through romantic 'rose-tinted' glasses. As romantic fiction writer Josephine Cox pointed out in Chapter 1, romantic love has a lot to answer for. M Scott Peck, the widely acclaimed psychiatrist and author of multi-million-selling book *The Road Less Travelled* writes: *"The myth of romantic love is a dreadful lie."* Scientists are even bigger spoilsports and killjoys when it comes to defining love. To them, love is 'merely' a couple's mutual addiction to a cocktail of hormones and chemicals such as oxytocin (also known as the love or cuddle hormone), serotonin (which affects our moods), opioids (a natural form of opium) and dopamine (sometimes referred to as 'the happy hormone').

So when you meet someone you really fancy, there's chemistry. Literally. What's going on inside are those chemicals specifically designed to get you to mate and reproduce. Although doing so would probably get you thrown out of a supermarket!

The point is, our purpose in life, from an evolutionary standpoint, is to reproduce, bond, protect and raise our children in a safe and stable family environment. That's why the first stage is invariably based on sexual attraction, or our 'Erotic Capital' as described by Dr Catherine Hakim, a senior sociology research fellow at the London School of Economics.

Falling head-over-heels for someone, being besotted, infatuated, the complete inability to see even the most basic incompatibilities, feeling unable to breathe, the cold sweats, an inability to speak, the butterflies in the stomach, the increased heart rate, the aching loins with added moistness or stiffness, euphoric lust, feeling light-headed, illogical and with the overwhelming desire to scream from the rooftops your dying, unconditional love and passion for this godlike creature you have just met is what we're talking about here. But how could this possibly be temporary? It is.

Am I suggesting you stop yourself? Are you kidding? Live your life. Enjoy every second of it while it lasts, but be aware that your entire body is trying to con you into mating: as often as possible, and with as many partners as you can find. There are always consequences though: emotionally and perhaps medically. And in a so-called 'civilised' society to do all of the above is also seen by religious groups, prudish parents (who probably did exactly the same themselves!) and society in general as being 'wrong'. So, succumb to pleasures of the flesh, and guilt or disapproval will often get out of bed with you, too.

You're not the first to struggle with this tension either. Hundreds of billions of other human beings throughout history have enjoyed or endured exactly the same.

What makes this type of all-consuming love so appealing is how it just happens to you. It doesn't require any effort. Then after a few months in a relationship, reality kicks in, the sex usually (but not always) becomes less important. For many, the sex is so appealing they don't seem to want to bother with the bonding, protecting and caring versions of 'love'. For them, when the passion subsides, they want another heady hit of those love hormones ASAP. So off they go to find a replacement partner to satisfy their short-term addiction for more romantic, sweep-you-off-your-feet 'love'. And to hell with who they hurt in the process.

Or if you're lucky to find someone with whom you share a deeper affection, you will stay together for the next phase of love. Before we gently caress the concept of real, long-lasting love, here are a few words about the various destructive forms of love.

Obsessive and Parasitic Love

In earlier chapters we discussed how some men and women create in their heads a fantasy of how life and love 'should' be. Then when reality doesn't conform to this, they often feel deeply unhappy. In some cases, they simply refuse to accept the reality. Locked into 'First Position' as described in the previous chapter, they see the situation only from their own perspective. In extreme cases they will bully, threaten, stalk and even physically attack the person they claim to 'love'. All because they cannot reconcile the difference between what the relationship 'should' be, with the reality of the situation for the other person. The movie *Fatal Attraction*, starring Michael Douglas and Glenn Close, is a chilling example of a woman who 'loves' so much she is prepared to kill in order to keep her man.

Only recently I had lunch with a friend who finally broke up with her long-term partner, after years of his attempts to control her. After the break-up he couldn't or wouldn't let her go. He would call at all hours and even bang on her front door in the middle of the night. Eventually she had no choice but to involve the police. Her former lover is now forbidden by law to come within 400 yards of her home. Who knows if he'll abide by this ruling? Scary stuff. It's relatively rare, but it does happen.

What obsessive lovers fail to accept is that no matter how they rationalise their behaviour, you cannot force anyone to love you. Ever. They often like to think of themselves as passionate, rather than obsessive. Because they have convinced themselves that they are experiencing deep, passionate love, they feel justified in using dirty tricks, manipulation and deceit to trap the object of their desire into a relationship the other person does not want. After all, in their view, it's for their lovers' own good, because who in their right mind could possibly turn down someone as wonderful as them? Whatever 'pure' motives they think they have, they are deluding themselves. They are not experiencing real love, they have just convinced themselves that it is.

A less scary, but nonetheless equally destructive form of love is Parasitic Love. Well known amongst psychiatrists and relationship counsellors, it's called 'Passive Dependent Personality Disorder'(PDPD). For sufferers of PDPD something feels missing from their lives. It's as if they possess a bottomless empty dark pit inside which they must constantly try to fill with anything or anyone.

Parasites live off their host. So long as someone, in fact anyone, is prepared to give them what they want, they will take whatever they can, for as long as that host serves their primary function. Those with PDPD don't really care about the needs of others. They just want to 'get'. 'Giving' is not part of their deal. This is another example of people locked into 'First Position'.

PDPD sufferers are so busy consuming 'love' there's nothing left to give. PDPD sufferers often aspire to being married to somebody who will satisfy all of their emotional needs. It doesn't even cross their minds that their own role is to care for the other person in equal measure. Because PDPD sufferers are so desperate for love, anyone in a relationship with such a person is often flattered into believing that they are being 'loved' so deeply. They are not. It isn't real love.

Anyone who behaves in any of the ways described in this section, regardless of how they try to justify it to themselves, cannot be The One for someone else. And they can't possibly be The One for you. Period.

True Love

Love is not a feeling, according to psychologist Erich Fromm in his book *The Art of Loving* (1956). Fromm, states that true love is based on an individual's ability and desire to care, respect, know and take responsibility for themselves and for others.

True love is a joint decision.

Once this decision is made, what each person chooses to do, day-to-day with and for their partner will determine the success of the relationship and the depth of that love.

This is echoed by psychiatrist M Scott Peck who defines love as: *"The will to extend one's self for the purpose of nurturing one's own or another's spiritual growth."* He accepts that this definition has its shortcomings and adds: *"True love is not a feeling by which we are overwhelmed. It is a committed, thoughtful decision."*

This means that true love involves effort. It's hard work, demanding constant attention from both parties. There are some who wrongly believe that if their current relationship starts to require effort, the love must have gone. So they dump a partner to start all over again. And again, and again. But in reality it hasn't actually been given the chance to start!

Hard physical work requires good fitness. The hard work of true love requires high levels of emotional fitness for both partners. And exercising it regularly.

Alternatively, you can stay together but abdicate responsibility for the well-being of the relationship. This approach increases the likelihood that the relationship will ultimately fail. Countless unhappily married people just fritter away their lives by not ending the relationship, but not working to improve it either. Taking a relationship for granted is a form of neglect.

So, what are some of the hallmarks of a healthy relationship that's based on true love? Both partners:

- have their own separate identities and interests.
- are happy that their partner is independent.
- are together through choice, rather than necessity.
- have deep mutual respect.
- care for one another's well-being.
- if their partner is ill or late returning from a trip, they will worry for their well-being.
- are joined by a commitment 'umbilical cord' (see next section).

- rely on and trust one another.
- fancy each other even after many years together.
- are prepared to listen and understand, rather than tell and assume.
- are mature and respectful when resolving conflicts.
- share roles and responsibilities equally, occasionally switching those roles.
- accept their differences and harness them to enhance the relationship.
- enjoy a life where they can be themselves in a relaxed and secure environment.
- face problems together, assuming joint responsibility for the solutions.
- are not in competition with each other.
- develop the habit of remembering to be loving to one another always, especially when they don't feel like it.
- are mutually supportive and encourage each other.
- still put each other first even when they have children together.
- have fun together because they really are each other's best friend.

If you're currently in a relationship, why not agree with each other to copy all the behaviours listed above (and any others you come up with together) and see what happens. Improvements are practically guaranteed: but only if you both do it.

The Role for Romance

So, if romantic love is not true love you might be asking whether romance has any part to play in a long-term, loving relationship? Of course it does.

However, there are different forms of romance. Firstly, there's obligatory romance: your partner's birthday, anniversary and of course Valentine's Day. Forgetting to buy a card or even the last, wilting bunch of flowers from the service station on your way home is unlikely to make your partner feel special. At the heart of romance is showing you still care, even if - especially if - you've been together for a long time. The 'once-in-a-blue-moon' grand gesture or something on 'special occasions' will never compare with a lot of smaller, unpredictable demonstrations that you are thinking lovingly of your partner.

A handwritten personal note left on the pillow when you've had to go away, doing something your partner will appreciate, an inexpensive 'perfect' gift with the words *"I saw this and thought of you"* are all seemingly insignificant gestures, yet the warmth they evoke will often last for years.

When it comes down to it, just like the layout of this chapter, you'll find that true love will grow when sandwiched between thick slices of 'trust' and 'commitment'.

C - Commitment

No matter what happens during life's journey, a couple who are truly committed to one another will work together in an equal partnership. They give and take equally. And share equal responsibility for the 'us'.

This commitment comes out of their deep mutual trust for one another. They know, based on past experiences together, that they are there for each other at all times. Their mutual commitment is a constant, the bedrock of that relationship. Without a solid commitment from both parties, their relationship has weak or non-existent foundations and is far more likely to collapse at some point.

Before we look closer at what it takes to be committed in a relationship, it's worth mentioning how and why some people can't or won't commit. Some are emotionally unavailable. For a variety of reasons they can't or won't commit to anyone. This may have absolutely nothing to do with you. Trying to convince them to change is usually futile. Indeed, the more you try, the more likely they will resist further. They may say they want to change, but words are cheap. Actions are the only proof. If you're with someone who is emotionally unavailable and you want to be in a mutually committed relationship, as tough as this might sound, you probably need to get out and find someone who is emotionally available.

Those suffering from psychiatric disorders often have massive issues with trust and commitment. Some degree of fear about commitment is actually a good thing though. It shows that the person is taking commitment seriously. It is a very big step. Anyone who claims they are prepared to commit relatively soon within a relationship, may not be taking it seriously enough. And if they try to persuade their partner to commit too soon, it could be a sign that they are fairly desperate to 'lock' that person into the relationship.

As well as emotional unavailability, these are just some of the other reasons why someone won't commit:

- an ongoing lack of trust.
- their own or their partner's underdeveloped Emotional Core.
- fear they will lose their independence and all the benefits that they perceive go with it.
- their relationship history: they've committed in the past and it went horribly wrong.
- fears that they might not be compatible long term.
- not being sure they share future goals and aspirations.
- a nagging, underlying sense that they're merely part of someone else's plan.

Telling each other you are committed is really easy. But true commitment is hard. Really hard. So a lot of people tend to prefer 'Commitment Lite'. It looks and tastes like the real thing but it's the diet cola variety, packed with artificial sweeteners and a stimulating cocktail of mood-altering chemicals which induce the illusion of love and intimacy.

What makes 'Commitment Lite' so appealing are its 'get out' clauses. There are loads of them. When you make a 'Commitment Lite' you can change your mind at any time. So any promises you make (or get told) can be withdrawn or ignored when it's not convenient. The side effects for 'Commitment Lite' are an underlying feeling of being slightly on edge, not quite sure if your partner is really committed to you. They say they are. But you're not sure. And they may have exactly the same thoughts and feelings.

Without open, ongoing communication neither party really knows where they stand with each other.

True commitment can only happen when two people trust each other implicitly, deeply confident that each person is determined to be there for the other person, every time. This form of commitment isn't based on guesswork or assumptions. You both know. Because over time, your actions have demonstrated it. Again and again. Commitment isn't emotional. It's another practical decision. In healthy relationships these factors are discussed openly and honestly. You've talked about it at length, you agree on the fundamentals of your relationship and you make promises to each other which you keep. True commitment to a higher-level relationship is founded on making this joint decision. As is the case with true love, this is a critically important factor. So look at your own attitude towards commitment.

- How often do you make promises to others, and also to yourself?
- How often do you break them?
- And how do you tend to rationalise or justify breaking those promises?

Become better at keeping every promise you make. There are only so many times broken promises will be accepted. Each broken promise chips something away from a relationship. So, whether you are in a relationship or not, develop the reputation for being someone who can be relied on to always do what they say. This starts with becoming more discerning and thoughtful about what promises you are prepared to make in the first place, and to whom. Take your promises more seriously. Don't make promises unless you are determined to fulfil them. Use Appendix I at the end of this book to make a promise to yourself. Accept that occasionally fulfilling a promise will mean personal sacrifices. Circumstances can and do change, but someone capable of being committed will always fulfil their promises. They don't let people down easily. And they certainly won't let down their partner unless it is absolutely unavoidable. A truly committed person's definition of 'unavoidable' will be vastly different to those who subscribe to 'Commitment Lite'.

If you promise to keep confidences, to care for each other, to respect one other, to support each other, to be loyal, to behave responsibly and remain faithful, you must keep those promises. If you can't or won't commit to any of these things, never say you will.

Committed people deliver on their promises consistently and over the long term, being and doing the best for each other - always.

Once men and women have experienced 'the moment' as described at the beginning of this book, they are more open to the idea of a long-term partner. It's worth remembering that stable, responsible men and women share the same fears, anxieties, dreams and aspirations, such as:

- to feel happy about who we are, where we are, and who we have decided to share our lives with.
- to have a fulfilling role: whether it's paid or voluntary work, or raising a family.
- to be liked by friends and colleagues.
- to feel deeply loved by family and partner/spouse. To be fully appreciated, supported, encouraged and respected by everyone who matters to us.
- to be with someone who is as committed to us, as we are to them.
- to enjoy a deep and mutually satisfying sexual relationship.
- to enjoy our leisure time, doing activities that we can be completely absorbed in.

- a life free of fear, insecurity and neediness and a life full of trust, kindness and friendship.
- to be part of an intimate team. Playing an equal role. Working together for the common good of the team. Enriching and improving each other's lives, sharing its ups and downs – together. Being a solid 'rock' for each other.
- and a shared sense of humour.

Stop and Start Reminders

Stop

- ☐ Stop insisting that everything must be perfect.
- ☐ Thinking that someone else must make you feel loved. No one else is responsible for your love.
- ☐ Let go of your disappointments.
- ☐ Forgive others as much as you would like them to forgive you.
- ☐ Some people, based on their past, are constantly seeking revenge with whomever they can take it out on. If that's you – stop.
- ☐ Every moment you think about any 'ex's' and what could have been is another moment stolen from your life.
- ☐ Don't keep score and don't expect everyone to return your favours. Sometimes people will take advantage of your generosity. Accept that now. Don't let it stop you being generous.
- ☐ Don't be too predictable.
- ☐ Stop being grumpy, whiney, sulky and miserable.
- ☐ Stop deliberately or accidentally making your partner dependent on you.
- ☐ Stop guessing. And most especially stop assuming. Ask questions instead.
- ☐ Accept things as they are not as you think you prefer them to be.
- ☐ Never fight with negative people. They have a habit of winning even when they lose. You will lose even when you win. Avoid them.
- ☐ Don't let a partner ever feel trapped.
- ☐ Staying together for a long time in a bad relationship isn't anything to be proud of. Either work to improve it or move on.
- ☐ The louder your voice, the less people will hear you.

- ☐ Stop feeling the need to impress others. You will invariably impress people more, the moment you decide you have nothing to prove.
- ☐ Don't pretend. Be.

Start

- ☐ Touch more, brush alongside your partner in a non-sexual way. Especially if you have children now or in the future, let them see you being affectionate. They will learn that open signs of affection are normal.
- ☐ Invest time, energy and attention in each other. Equally.
- ☐ Be curious about your partner. Look for a partner who is curious about life and has an enquiring open mind.
- ☐ Be curious yourself. Learn new things all the time.
- ☐ Time and time again people have said that they met somebody who they would otherwise dismiss as being completely unsuitable who ends up becoming the love of their life. Remember *When Harry Met Sally.*
- ☐ Be more open-minded.
- ☐ Be courteous. Politeness will never go out of fashion.
- ☐ No relationship you have is more important than the one you have with your partner. Not even your relationship with your children, although they may be as important to you, in a different way of course. Never neglect your partner simply because children (or other family) are making demands. You and your partner must remain the rock for any children.
- ☐ Constantly focus on what's great about your partner and why you love them.
- ☐ Celebrate the success of others.
- ☐ Show appreciation on a daily basis.
- ☐ Say "*yes*" to more opportunities.
- ☐ Learn to be patient. Slow down.
- ☐ Simplify your life.
- ☐ Look around your home at all the 'stuff' you have accumulated. Our lives are full of 'what seemed like a good idea at the time'. Get rid of clutter in your life.

- ☐ It is very difficult to feel calm and at peace if you are surrounded with clutter. Turn your home into a calm sanctuary. A place where you can relax.
- ☐ Plant seeds of potential and hope in other people, especially a partner.
- ☐ Demonstrate how much you care. Prove it, don't just say it.
- ☐ When you think of your disappointments and failures, do so only briefly. And then think about how you successfully overcame those situations. You have what it takes to deal with all of life's obstacles.
- ☐ Improve the existing relationships you have with family and friends. Make it a priority. Get used to being proactive about relationships.
- ☐ Always keep your friendships alive.
- ☐ Decide to become a full version of you.
- ☐ Learn to relax when you hug. A 'real' hug makes you feel as though you're melting into each other: in a non-sexual way.
- ☐ Never hugged your parents before? Without making a big thing of it, sidle up to them one day and give them a hug. Don't talk yourself out of it, especially if it hasn't been something you've done in the past.
- ☐ Tell the people who you care about how you feel about them. Look them in the eye when you say it. Or if this is too far out of your comfort zone drop them a note or an e-mail. If you feel awkward expressing your emotions with others, you need practice. Each time you reach out it will become easier. Consider this an affection training course. This training will prove invaluable when you meet The One.
- ☐ When you keep thinking the same thoughts, you reinforce the neural pathways in your brain. The question is: do those thoughts help you or hinder you? Think positive thoughts.

- ☐ Forgive those who are doing their best, even if they don't measure up to your standards.
- ☐ Look forward to more things. Make a point of spending at least some time looking forward to each of the activities that you have put into your diary. This can be anything from a day trip, going to the movies or meeting up with friends.
- ☐ Even the most powerful force on this planet ebbs and flows every day. Be like the tides. Give and take from your partner in equal measure.
- ☐ Problems never get smaller if they're left to sort themselves out. Be proactive.
- ☐ See more in others than they see in themselves.
- ☐ Think more about being a good partner yourself, rather than questioning whether your partner is any good.
- ☐ Forgive your partner for what you see are their shortcomings – in truth, it could be that you have a bigger shortcoming by being so critical/judgemental about them!
- ☐ You need to have and to be a shoulder to cry on.
- ☐ Listen by giving your full attention regardless of circumstances.
- ☐ No matter how long you've been together, schedule regular dates with each other.
- ☐ Make a point of saying complimentary things about and to each other.
- ☐ Decide what you want to do together in the future. Then together, create those plans so they become a shared aspiration and you will both look forward equally to enjoying them.
- ☐ Revisit those special places you enjoyed together.
- ☐ Let them know you are really pleased to see them. Every time.

Chapter 12

And Finally...

- One workout session won't get you physically fit.
- One shower won't keep you clean.
- One housekeeping session won't keep your home clean and tidy.

Some things need to be repeated for any lasting benefits. *How to Be The One* is such a project. Emotional fitness is an investment of your time.

Focusing on your Emotional Core is a bit like adding oxygen to glowing embers. Combustion takes place and flames will appear, seemingly out of nowhere. From the darkness, you will start to radiate genuine light and warmth.

With a strong Emotional Core you don't 'need' anyone. Because you like yourself and realise that not just anyone will do, this means you are more selective about who you choose to get involved with. You trust yourself more. You won't tolerate those who try to control, bully or use you. You know that you have the inner strength to walk away from anyone who messes you around, puts you down, is disrespectful or treats you badly in any other way.

Maintaining your Emotional Core is a never-ending process. It requires at least some conscious awareness and mindfulness. It's about remembering to look after yourself, maintaining your self-esteem and a more appealing attitude. It's a reminder to you to appreciate what you have in your life right now. This will encourage you to feel happier about yourself, therefore making you more likely to treat others kindly and compassionately. Improvements like these provide the best preparation for all forms of future intimacy.

So let me remind you about the suggestions made at the beginning of this book: flick back over the pages to remind yourself of what you found most relevant. Decide which elements will be your future focus. The more you remind yourself that you are a good person, that you have the qualities people find appealing, the more likely it becomes that others will sense that. So make a promise to yourself to work on those areas of your life. Sign and date Appendix 1, your personal contract. Don't try to do everything all at once; choose three or four areas to work on at a time. Add more at a later date, as you make progress. Don't ever allow yourself to feel overwhelmed if you feel you have a lot to do. Move slowly and steadily towards a strong Emotional Core, one day at a time. There's no rush. Take small steps. Don't be tempted to take any short cuts. Because there aren't any.

Make regular appointments with yourself to study the Stop and Start Reminders you marked. Make these daily routines, your new empowering habits. Write down how you feel today, and then make an appointment in three months and again in six months to review your progress. When you revisit these pages, notice any changes and improvements you feel about yourself. Discuss what you have learned with your partner or any of your friends who, like you, take relationships seriously. Help each other.

All too often women complain that men don't bother to understand women enough. And in some cases it is probably true. However, I've asked many of the women I know whether they have ever taken even a moment to truly understand what it must be like to be a man in today's society. In more than 90%

of cases this question produces a long silence, before a quiet admission that she has never actually done that.

And guys: really try to understand the pressures woman face and what it must be like juggling all sorts of work and family responsibilities. Life is increasingly difficult for men as well as for women. These difficulties are different for each gender. Remind yourself of that as often as you can.

It's far too easy to assume that men have all the advantages and that women don't. Lots of men think it's women who have the easy life. Neither is true.

However, this **is** true: women have far better developed vocabularies when it comes to articulating their emotions. Guys want true intimacy, too, but are often completely at a loss to know how to express their emotions accurately. That doesn't make them knuckle-dragging Neanderthals!

As we come to the end of this book, let me share a true story about Glyn, my middle brother. His mates call him a *'Jedi'*. Not because he's a *Star Wars* fan but because he is particularly wise, a devoted father, a mountaineer and a survival specialist. He's the sort of guy you'd really want to be with if you found yourself in an extreme situation.

Glyn was studying for a university degree as a mature student (having been written off as a 'no-hoper' whilst at school). The lecturer had asked the class to think of the five most important people in their lives and wanted a volunteer to share their choices. Everyone else was too shy, so Glyn stepped forward. When he reached the front, he froze and said:

> *"I've just noticed that the one person who isn't on my list, is the most important person in my life: Jill, my wife. That has shocked me a bit. But I've now just realised why she isn't on my list. Quite seriously, she is me. I am her."*

That's what it's like for some people when you are each married to The One.

Appendix 1

Personal Contract and Promise

I, (your name).. promise myself to commit to becoming the best person I can be for myself and the one person I choose to be with. I accept that to live first class, with a first class partner I need to be committed to doing everything in my power to be a first class person myself.

This means I will identify areas of my behaviour and personality that will be most likely to benefit from a makeover or an upgrade. I will look after myself and learn to become emotionally fit. In order to be successful and achieving these improvements I accept that it will involve effort on my part and the support of trusted friends and family members. I will invite my closest friends to support me. Simultaneously, I will offer the same level of support and encouragement to those who support me - in the ways they most want my support.

I accept myself for who I am today. I will be kind to myself and others as I move towards adopting and absorbing new and more appealing qualities to make me a truly irresistible human being.

....

Your signature date

Appendix 2

How to Turn Off a Woman

- Poor personal hygiene – body odour, dirty finger nails, bad breath, dirty teeth, nose picking. Constantly adjusting your crotch. Gross acts that would turn off anyone. Unless of course they too had exactly the same habits. Then, of course it's a perfect match for soul-mate slobs.
- Poor personal grooming. Badly scuffed shoes. Frayed collars and cuffs. Leftovers from past meals on their clothes. One for the older men – untrimmed nose and ear hair! These are all signs that you don't look after yourself. To many women this means it's very unlikely that you will look after her either.
- Unreliability. Failing to show up or being late regularly.
- Bragging. Trying to impress by saying how clever you are, how much money you earn, how much everyone likes you, the car(s) you drive. How big your TV is etc. High-quality women are not impressed. Gold-diggers are.
- Self-obsession. A variation of bragging. It's all - Me me me. Just about everything they say revolves around them. How wonderful they are. Who they know. What people say about them. Who said what to whom. To them, a conversation is 'I talk. You listen'. They just want an audience. Best summarised with this funny quote from Bette Midler in the movie 'Beaches' - *"Enough about me. Tell me. What do you think of me?"*
- Disrespect to others. For example, they treat waiters and waitresses as 'sub-humans' thinking they are being clever or cool by being dismissive. Waiting staff will tell you that ANYONE who ever clicks their fingers to attract their attention will not be looked after properly. Potential partners are extremely observant about how their date treats everybody else they come into contact with when they are together. It's one of the most accurate signs of how that person will end up treating them.

Appendix 3

How to Turn Off a Man

- Be needy. Neediness is the biggest turn-off by far, for any man who is emotionally stable and normal. However, neediness is very appealing to men who have their own lack of self-confidence and are looking for somebody they can control in order to give themselves a feeling of self-importance. Do you really want somebody like that in your life? Find any way you can to stop being emotionally needy today! Don't just look as if you're not needy, become genuinely non-needy.
- General sulking and grumpiness. Men will tell you that they may have had male friends for years, even decades – who have NEVER sulked with them. They'll tell you only women do this.
- Any form of psychological game playing.
- Expecting him to pay for everything. Most men are happy to 'treat' women. It makes them feel good. However, a woman who never offers to contribute, or even to volunteer to pay the tip occasionally won't last long.
- Being a tease. Flirting is good. Sexual teasing is not. Except of course, if you are already together in a good relationship: teasing that eventually 'delivers' can be incredible for both parties.
- Expecting sex to be 'done' to you. It's a 'with you' activity.
- Expecting a guy to have telepathic powers or to understand female subtlety. They don't, can't and won't.

About Roy Sheppard

For decades Roy has brought people together. He is also a former BBC television and radio presenter and reporter, as well as a visiting lecturer on Cranfield School of Management's full time MBA course in England.

As a journalist, he has written for national newspapers and magazines and interviewed countless global business leaders, politicians and celebrities. He is author of the following books; *Your Personal Survival Guide to the 21st Century* (out of print), *Meet, Greet and Prosper*, *Rapid Result Referrals* and the audio programs *The Secrets of Successful Freelancing* and *Network to Win*. He is the co-author of a serious study about how to spot and protect yourself against dangerous women. His co-author Mary T Cleary is a world authority on the subject of male victims of domestic violence. *Venus: The Dark Side* and *That Bitch: Protect Yourself Against Women with Malicious Intent* are the same books.

Today Roy works as a highly-acclaimed conference moderator, often chairing complex, unscripted discussions to resolve differences and challenges inside and outside many of the world's largest and most successful organisations.

www.RoySpeaks.com
www.YouTube.com/RoySheppard
www.Twitter.com/RoySheppard
Join our How to Be The One Facebook fan page.

Charity Donation

A percentage of the net profits from this book will be donated to Tools for Self Reliance, a UK based charity supported by the author.

For thirty years, Tools for Self Reliance has helped relieve poverty in Africa by supporting small businesses and by raising awareness in the UK. With the help of hundreds of dedicated volunteers in the UK, and partner organisations in Africa, Tools for Self Reliance provides business skills and other training projects in six African countries. And each year Tools for Self Reliance ships tens of thousands of refurbished tools and sewing machines to Africa and puts them into the hands of people who really need them. www.tfsr.org

Other Books by Roy Sheppard

The Daily Stop and Start Reminders from *How to Be The One* in a handy pocket book format to carry around with you in your pocket or bag.

Now you can remind yourself each day to absorb the specific qualities and behaviours you want to adopt as part of the new you. 64 pages.

Only available by mail order.
Visit www.CentrePublishing.com.

Do you brighten a room when you walk in - or when you leave? What mistakes do you unwittingly make when meeting and greeting strangers?

This handy book of pocket wisdom offers answers to those questions and many more together with hundreds of practical tips and ideas.

To order these titles and others
visit www.CentrePublishing.com
or your preferred bookshop.

How to Spot a Dangerous Woman

Please note: these titles are **exactly** the same book.

Men and women from all over the world have applauded the authors for daring to write so knowledgeably about this taboo topic. Nasty and malicious women dislike this book intensely because for the first time, their antics have been described so clearly. Forensically written, it provides detailed information on how to recognise the minority of women who will stop at nothing to destroy the lives and reputations of innocent men and women. It offers practical guidance on what you can do if you have been targeted, before it's too late. Co-written with Mary T Cleary, a world authority on the subject of male victims of domestic abuse and the founder of www.Amen.ie.

"..the authors are to be commended for having the guts to state the truth."
"...it treads boldly into areas that society likes to ignore and mock."
"Essential Guide for Men and Women."
"...discusses an important phenomenon of the modern era - the unscrupulous woman who uses the protection of the family and criminal law systems as a way to plunder men."

A New Fun Way to Show Your Appreciation

When you see someone who evokes a 'Wow!!' just pass them one of these fun cards.

On the back of each card it says:

"Something special about you has compelled someone to give you this 'wow'. Pass on this card or keep it to remind yourself that you have been appreciated."

(space below for a personal message)

"Remember – the card giver can't talk to you unless you choose to talk to them."

For more information or to order inexpensive packs of these cards visit www.WowCardz.com